MW01091823

the NEW FRENCH KITCHEN

Modern Takes on
Favorite Classic Dishes

GÉRALDINE LEVERD

ROCK
POINT

À ma maman.
(To my mom.)

CONTENTS

INTRODUCTION

French Cuisine with a Modern Take

I know what you're thinking: Is this another book on French cuisine with delicious, fancy recipes that I could never make on a daily basis?

Even though I'm a huge fan of traditional French cuisine, well, that's not what you'll find in this cookbook. I want to show that French cuisine can be easy, quick, and healthy, all at the same time. I've chosen some simple classic French dishes that I love for their freshness and ease of preparation, as well as twists on recipes that are now commonplace in modern French gastronomy. I've also included numerous vegetarian recipes to cater to a more flexitarian and environmentally friendly diet.

The goal of this book is to provide you with inspiration for everyday meals that you can include in your weekly planning. For me, cooking is also about sharing, and I love hosting. So, I've also included relatively easy-to-make recipes that are perfect for impressing your guests without spending the entire evening in the kitchen.

A Little about Me

I was born in Paris, France, and grew up in a small, peaceful, and green town near the capital. It was at home that I discovered my passion for homemade dishes. Despite a busy schedule, my mom always found the time to prepare a warm meal with fresh ingredients every evening, cooking us easy and healthy recipes. Soon, I started helping her in the kitchen, developing my creativity and love for this special time of the day.

As I grew up and pursued my studies and a career, my commitment to healthy, homemade cooking remained strong. Over time, I noticed a real need for inspiration for quick and balanced everyday meals among those around me. This is how I began sharing my everyday recipes inspired by French cuisine on social media, followed by starting a food blog. With content initially intended for my friends and family, my desire to share my culinary creations quickly attracted a growing community. Without this incredible community, I wouldn't be writing the introduction to my first cookbook today! In 2023, I made a big decision to turn this passion into my profession. Today, I am able to live from my activities as a recipe developer, content creator, and food photographer.

How to Use This Book

I organized the recipes in this book for easy navigation, whether you are planning a weeknight dinner or a weekend dinner party!

APPETIZERS AND STARTERS

In France, welcoming guests often begins with an aperitif in which small dishes are served to be enjoyed, followed by a starter before the main course. Personally, I like simply serving shared appetizers or starters in the center of the table on one plate, allowing everyone to enjoy a bit of everything in a convivial way. The Summer Tapenades (page 22) and Whipped Brown Butter with Espelette Pepper (page 41) are must-tries!

SOUPS

Soups are often served as a starter in France no matter the time of year. I love soups because they can be adapted depending on what's in season and what you have on hand. In winter, nothing beats a comforting bowl of Rustic Vegetable Soup

(page 55), while in warmer months, lighter options can be enjoyed, such as Chilled Zucchini and Pea Soup (page 44) and Fish Soup with Fennel and Orange (page 52) .

SALADS

You can always find a salad option on a French menu, whether served as a starter or a main course. In this book, I've included some classics, such as the timeless Parisian bistro favorite with a twist, Warm Goat Cheese and Strawberry Salad (page 61) and a winter favorite, Endive Salad with Orange, Cheese, and Walnuts (page 58). You'll also discover some of my own creations, including my personal favorite, Pea Salad with Mint and Smoked Salmon (page 65).

MEAT MAINS

In France, meat dishes often take center stage, whether for a casual family dinner or a special occasion. In this book, I wanted to share some of my favorite dishes that are perfect for both everyday meals and when hosting guests. For a cozy family dinner, try the One-Pan Stuffed Tomatoes à la Provençale with Rice (page 80), an easy and flavorful option. If you're looking for something special when having guests over, the Braised Beef with Red Wine and Carrots (page 97) and Herbed Bacon-Wrapped Pork Tenderloin (page 87) are sure to impress.

FISH MAINS

Fish is a staple in my kitchen, and it's something I love to cook regularly. If you find cooking fish a bit intimidating, these recipes are here to guide you, offering simple steps with delicious results. From the bold flavors of Tuna Steak with Tomato, Olives, and Capers (page 117) to the vibrant Baked Salmon with Almond, Olive, and Preserved Lemon Salsa (page 113), there's something for every taste.

VEGETARIAN MAINS

Traditionally, French cuisine hasn't been known for its vegetarian options, but that's beginning to change. Even in France, more people are embracing a flexitarian lifestyle, incorporating plant-forward dishes into their everyday meals. In this section, I've included some of my favorite vegetarian recipes that are perfect for dinner. You'll find delicious quiches, such as the Swiss Chard and Mushroom Quiche with Buckwheat Shortcrust Pastry (page 131) and the light and refreshing Zucchini, Mint, and Ricotta Quiche (page 151). I've also reimagined some classic French dishes, such as the Vegetarian Lentil and Eggplant Parmentier (page 129), offering a hearty, meat-free twist on a beloved favorite.

SIDE DISHES

In this book, side dishes aren't just an afterthought—they often play a starring role in the meal! As a vegetable lover, I've carefully selected some standout sides that will elevate any menu. You simply have to try the Green Beans with Crunchy Honey Almonds (page 163) and the flavorful Roasted Fennel with Arugula Pesto (page 159). Of course, I couldn't resist including a few classics, such as Healthy Oven-Baked French Fries (page 160) and Slow-Roasted Vegetable Ratatouille (page 168), which pair beautifully with nearly every recipe in this book.

DESSERTS

In France, almost every meal ends with a dessert. In this book, I have included some of my favorites for every season, from the Classic Apple Tarte Tatin (page 191) and Chocolate Fondants (page 175), to revisited classics, such as Crème Brûlée with Orange and Cardamom (page 179), to lighter options, such as Roasted Peaches with Yogurt Ice Cream and Toasted Buckwheat (page 187). So, make sure you reserve some space so you don't miss out on the best part (well, almost the best part) of a dinner!!

THE FRENCH PANTRY

These are the ingredients I use daily in my cooking and in the recipes throughout this book.

Oil

It is crucial to equip yourself with high-quality olive oils. For salads, vinaigrettes, and other raw dishes, I prefer extra-virgin olive oil with a robust flavor to really enhance the taste. Whenever possible, I opt for AOP olive oils, which are certified Protected Designation of Origin from specific regions, such as AOP Huile d'Olive de Nyons or AOP Huile d'Olive de Provence. (For vinaigrettes, I sometimes vary oils by using walnut, hazelnut, or rapeseed oil.) For cooking, a more neutral and affordable extra-virgin olive oil is perfect for sautéing and roasting.

NOTE: Contrary to some beliefs, olive oil can indeed be used for cooking, depending on its quality and smoke point—the temperature at which it starts to emit smoke. For extra-virgin olive oil, the smoke point ranges from 320°F (160°C) to 410°F (210°C) and can reach 390°F (200°C) to 475°F (245°C) for refined olive oil.

Vinegar

I generally use either white wine or red wine vinegar. In some recipes, I like to use balsamic vinegar to enhance the flavor and add depth to dishes, especially in tomato sauces and on roasted vegetables. When I mention balsamic vinegar, I am referring to the syrupy balsamic vinegar made from grape must, such as Modena DOP vinegar.

Butter

Of course, when you think of French cuisine, you think of butter! And if you ask the Bretons, from Brittany, they will tell you there is only one kind of butter: salted butter. Personally, I like to use either unsalted or salted butter depending on the recipe. Unless otherwise indicated, all the recipes with butter in this book use unsalted butter. Traditional French butter contains at least 82 percent milk fat.

HOMEMADE SALTED BUTTER

This is so simple to make! All you need is some high-quality unsalted butter and sea salt flakes, preferably fleur de sel (page 10).

Let the butter sit at room temperature for at least 30 minutes. Place the butter in a medium bowl and add between 0.5 to 3 percent of the butter weight in sea salt (for example, if you are using 100 grams of butter, you would add between 0.5 to 3 grams of salt). Using a fork, incorporate the salt into the butter, whipping it slightly. Transfer the butter to a butter dish or wrap it in parchment paper, shaping it into a log. It can be stored in the refrigerator just like regular butter.

Cream

In French cuisine, cream, like butter, is a fundamental ingredient in many recipes, and we commonly use three types: crème fraîche, crème liquid, and crème fleurette.

CRÈME FRAÎCHE

Crème fraîche is a thick, cultured cream with a rich, tangy flavor. It's similar to sour cream but has a higher fat content and a smoother texture. It is often used in sauces, soups, and desserts to add a luxurious creaminess. Nowadays, you can find crème fraiche at most grocery stores; if not, you can make your own by mixing heavy whipping cream with a bit of buttermilk and letting it sit at room temperature until thickened.

CRÈME LIQUIDE

Crème liquide, or liquid cream, typically refers to heavy whipping cream. It's a versatile ingredient used for both cooking and baking. In France, crème liquide can be found in various fat percentages, but for most recipes, I recommend using one with at least 30 percent fat.

CRÈME FLEURETTE

Crème fleurette is a cream that is typically fresher and thinner than crème liquide. It is often unpasteurized or minimally pasteurized, which preserves its delicate flavor and makes it ideal for whipping, such as for Chantilly Cream (page 188) or for use in delicate desserts. The main difference between crème liquide and crème fleurette is that crème fleurette is usually richer and more flavorful due to its minimal processing.

Salt

Salt is an indispensable ingredient in French cuisine. There are two primary salts I rely on: table salt and fleur de sel.

TABLE SALT

Table salt is the most commonly used variety. It can be iodized, non-iodized, or even sea salt. I use this salt regularly as a foundational element in all my recipes. Unless otherwise indicated, if only "salt" is listed in the ingredient list of a recipe, use table salt.

FLEUR DE SEL

Fleur de sel is a special salt that I reserve exclusively for finishing dishes such as roasted vegetables, grilled meats, and salads. It is a high-quality sea salt, hand-harvested from the surface of salt marshes. Fleur de sel is characterized by delicate crystals and a nuanced, complex flavor profile that differs from table salt. For a substitute, you can use sea salt flakes.

Black Pepper

In French cuisine, black pepper is a staple that is used for spicing up dishes. You'll notice that I top off almost all my recipes with a few twists of the pepper mill. Personally, I find that freshly ground pepper packs a much more intense flavor than store-bought ground pepper, so here's a recommendation that makes all the difference in cooking: Don't hesitate to invest in a pepper mill and black peppercorns.

Herbs

Herbs are essential in French cuisine, bringing aroma and flavor to many dishes. Whether fresh, aromatic, or dried, 90 percent of the recipes in this book include an herb!

FRESH HERBS

Fresh herbs are essential for enhancing the flavor and freshness of dishes. Among the most commonly used in French cuisine are parsley, chives, thyme, rosemary, basil, and tarragon. I generally add them toward the end of cooking or as a garnish.

DRIED HERBS

Most fresh herbs are also available dried. I generally use dried herbs for cooking rather than garnish, as they release their flavor best when heated. Additionally, I find that the texture is less appealing if they are not cooked. Be careful when substituting dried herbs for fresh ones, and vice versa, as dried herbs have a much more intense flavor, so you may need to reduce the amount.

HERBES DE PROVENCE

Herbes de Provence is a blend of dried herbs from the region of Provence. It is used when making sauces, seasoning vegetables for roasting, and marinating. Here's how to make your own blend:

YIELD 10½ tablespoons

PREP TIME 5 minutes

---

3 tablespoons dried thyme

2 tablespoons dried savory

2 tablespoons dried marjoram

1½ tablespoons dried rosemary

1 tablespoon dried oregano

1 tablespoon dried basil

In a small bowl, mix all the herbs until well combined, then transfer to a small glass jar. Tightly seal the lid and store in a dry place protected from light. It will keep for several years. You will find some blends that include lavender or sage, so feel free to experiment with your blend of herbs.

NOTE: You'll see "bouquet garni" mentioned in a few recipes. This is simply an assortment of herbs, traditionally composed of thyme, bay leaf, parsley (especially the stems), and sometimes rosemary tied together with kitchen string. It is added to soups, stews, and sauces to flavor them. Because the herbs are wrapped together, the bouquet garni can easily be removed before serving the dish.

Dijon Mustard

Dijon mustard is a classic condiment from Dijon in the Burgundy region of France that is known for its tangy, sharp flavor. It comes in both smooth and whole grain varieties. The smooth type blends seamlessly into dishes, offering a uniform flavor, while the whole grain version not only adds a delightful crunch, but it is also milder in taste. The grains remain intact because they are not fully ground, which makes this version perfect for enhancing the texture of dressings and meat toppings. I love to use Dijon in many recipes, especially vinaigrette dressings, marinades, sauces, and dips. If you cannot find Dijon or don't have any on hand, use yellow mustard mixed with a splash of white wine vinegar.

Piment d'Espelette

Piment d'Espelette, or Espelette pepper, is an iconic spice from the French Basque Country. It is a mild pepper with a subtle, spicy flavor and has become popular to use in modern French cuisine for enhancing dishes without masking their flavors. Its spiciness is rated at approximately 4 on the Scoville scale. Exclusively cultivated in the region of Espelette in the Basque Country, piment d'Espelette has both an Appellation d'Origine Contrôlée (AOC) and an Appellation d'Origine Protégée (AOP), ensuring its authenticity and quality. You can find it in stores specializing in French cuisine.

Piment d'Espelette has no true equivalent in terms of flavor. However, you can create a similar spice by mixing 1 tablespoon of smoked paprika, 2 tablespoons of sweet paprika, and 1 teaspoon of cayenne pepper. This blend will replicate the mild sweetness and subtle spiciness of piment d'Espelette, although its unique taste remains unmatched. In some recipes, I have indicated to substitute cayenne pepper, but be sure to use less than the amount suggested for the Espelette pepper, as cayenne pepper has more heat.

THE BASICS

Before diving into the recipes, I'd like to share four essential basics, along with some variations, that I use frequently. They will help you easily adapt and customize your weekly meal plans.

Vinaigrette

Here's my basic vinaigrette recipe, which is the perfect ratio for me. Many recipes call for a 3:1 oil-to-vinegar ratio, which is also what you learn in culinary school, but I often find that to be too oily. I prefer a sharper vinaigrette with a 2:1 oil-to-vinegar ratio. So, if you're like me and enjoy a strong vinaigrette, or if you're still figuring out your preference, try this ratio first. If the taste is too strong, you can always add 1 to 2 more tablespoons of olive oil. This rule applies to all the vinaigrette recipes in this book. Here's an additional tip: if this ratio is too acidic for your taste, try adding 1 teaspoon of honey; it will reduce the acidity, and you may not need to add any additional oil. Here's the recipe:

YIELD About ½ cup (120 ml)

PREP TIME 5 minutes
___

1 teaspoon Dijon mustard

2 tablespoons red wine vinegar

¼ cup (60 ml) olive oil

Salt and black pepper

¼ medium shallot, diced (optional)
___

In a small bowl, whisk together the Dijon mustard and red wine vinegar. Gradually add the olive oil while continuously whisking until well blended, to create an emulsion. The mixture should thicken and become smooth. Season with salt and pepper. If using, add the diced shallot. (The shallot and red wine combination is a classic, perfect to serve with a green salad.)

NOTE: In France, we always serve a green salad alongside the cheese plate, which comes after the main course and before dessert.

Here are ways you can vary your vinaigrette:

- **USE DIFFERENT OILS AND ALTERNATIVE VINEGARS:** Replace the olive oil with walnut, rapeseed, or avocado oil for a different flavor. Substitute the red or white wine vinegar with lemon juice or fruity vinegars, such as raspberry vinegar.

- **ADD SWEETNESS:** Add a touch of honey or maple syrup for sweetness.

- **MIX IN GARLIC:** Include minced garlic for an extra kick.

- **INCLUDE FRESH HERBS:** Fresh herbs like parsley, basil, or thyme can add a burst of flavor.

- **FLAVOR WITH FRUIT:** Incorporate crushed fruits like strawberries, raspberries, or figs.

Mayonnaise

Mayonnaise is an essential condiment in French cuisine that is used in many dishes, such as sandwiches, salads, and dips. It also forms the basis of many sauces and dressings, such as aioli, tartar sauce, and the rouille sauce served in bouillabaisse. Here's how to make it yourself:

YIELD 1 cup (240 ml)

PREP TIME 10 minutes
___

1 tablespoon Dijon mustard

1 tablespoon fresh lemon juice
or apple cider vinegar

1 medium egg yolk

1 pinch salt

1 cup (240 ml) oil (sunflower, canola, or olive)
___

In a medium bowl, whisk together the mustard, lemon juice, egg yolk, and salt for a few seconds to incorporate the ingredients well. Start adding the oil gradually, a drizzle at a time, while continuously whisking (it is important to pour the oil slowly to allow the mixture to thicken properly). Continue adding the oil gradually while whisking until all the oil is incorporated and the mayonnaise has reached a thick and creamy consistency. Transfer to an airtight container and store in the refrigerator for up to 1 week.

NOTES: Remove all the ingredients from the refrigerator 15 minutes before making the mayonnaise.

For a healthier version, mix the finished mayonnaise with ⅔ cup (160 ml) plain Greek yogurt and a pinch of salt.

Shortcrust Pastry for Quiche and Tarts

Shortcrust pastry is a fundamental element in French cuisine and plays a key role in this book. It can be used for both savory quiches and sweet tarts. I've developed six variations of the classic shortcrust pastry to suit different ingredients you might have at home.

Here are ways you can vary your shortcrust pastry:

- **USE DIFFERENT FLOURS**: Varying the flour can really transform your shortcrust pastry. Keep in mind that some flours, such as buckwheat, absorb more water. If your dough feels too crumbly, it's a sign to add a bit more water.

- **ADD DRIED HERBS:** I love adding herbs, especially for quiches. Dried thyme, rosemary, basil, or herbes de Provence can bring wonderful flavors to your dough.

Classic Shortcrust Pastry

PÂTE BRISÉE CLASSIQUE

This is the classic and authentic shortcrust pastry recipe. It is versatile and can be used for both savory dishes like quiches and sweet desserts.

WEIGHT About 12 ounces (360 g)
TART PAN SIZE 11 inches (28 cm)
RECIPE Classic Apple Tarte Tatin (page 191)

1 cup plus ⅔ cup (200 g) all-purpose flour
½ teaspoon (3 g) salt
3½ ounces (100 g) unsalted butter, at room temperature
1 medium egg yolk
3 tablespoons (45 ml) water

———
See instructions on page 15.

NOTE: This recipe is wonderful, but sometimes, I prefer not to "lose" an egg white. When I make this recipe for quiche, I add the remaining egg white into the egg batter for extra protein, even if the recipe doesn't call for it.

Shortcrust Pastry with Whole Egg

PÂTE BRISÉE AVEC ŒUF ENTIER

This is a great alternative to the Classic Shortcrust Pastry if you don't want to waste an egg white and prefer using a whole egg.

WEIGHT About 12 ounces (360 g)
TART PAN SIZE 11 inches (28 cm)
RECIPE Vegetable Quiche Tian-Style (page 136; I add dried thyme to this shortcrust pastry)

———
1 cup plus ⅔ cup (200 g) all-purpose flour
3½ ounces (100 g) unsalted butter, at room temperature
½ teaspoon (3 g) salt
1 medium egg
1 tablespoon (15 ml) water

———
See instructions on page 15.

Shortcrust Pastry without Egg
PÂTE BRISÉE SANS ŒUF

This recipe is ideal if you don't have any eggs or don't have enough for the dough. If you replace the butter with a plant-based alternative, you can easily make a vegan shortcrust pastry.

WEIGHT about 12 ounces (360 g)

TART PAN SIZE 11 inches (28 cm)

RECIPE Salmon and Leek Quiche (page 118)

———

1 cup plus ⅔ cup (200 g) all-purpose flour

3½ ounces (100 g) unsalted butter, at room temperature

½ teaspoon (3 g) salt

¼ cup (60 ml) cold water

———

See instructions opposite.

Olive Oil Shortcrust Pastry
PÂTE BRISÉE À L'HUILE D'OLIVE

This is a great dairy-free option.

WEIGHT About 11½ ounces (330 g)

TART PAN SIZE 11 inches (28 cm)

RECIPE Zucchini, Mint, and Ricotta Quiche (page 151) and Swiss Chard and Mushroom Quiche with Buckwheat Shortcrust Pastry (page 131; in this recipe, I replace some of the flour with buckwheat flour)

———

1 cup plus ⅔ cup (200 g) all-purpose flour

½ teaspoon (3 g) salt

1 medium egg

¼ cup (60 ml) olive oil

2 tablespoons (30 ml) cold water

———

See instructions opposite.

Yogurt Shortcrust Pastry
PÂTE BRISÉE AU YAOURT

This recipe is a healthier alternative using yogurt instead of butter or olive oil.

WEIGHT About 12 ounces (360 g)

TART PAN SIZE 11 inches (28 cm)

RECIPE Arugula, Cherry Tomato, and Feta Quiche (page 144)

———

1 cup plus ⅔ cup (200 g) all-purpose flour

½ teaspoon (3 g) salt

⅓ cup plus 1 tablespoon (100 g) plain yogurt (3.5% fat)

1 medium egg

1 tablespoon (15 ml) water

———

See instructions opposite.

Sweet Shortcrust Pastry
PÂTE BRISÉE SUCRÉE

I like to use this dough to make tarts with fruit, especially when the fruit is naturally tart, such as apricots or plums.

WEIGHT About 14 ounces (400 g)

TART PAN SIZE 11 inches (28 cm)

RECIPE: Apricot, Almond, and Pistachio Tart (page 176)

———

1 cup plus ⅔ cup (200 g) all-purpose flour

¼ cup (50 g) of caster sugar

1 pinch salt

3½ ounces (100 g) unsalted butter, at room temperature

1 medium egg

———

See instructions opposite.

NOTE: For all recipes in this book that require baking, I suggest using the convection setting on your oven, as it uses less energy because the fan helps the air circulate. If your oven doesn't have this setting, increase the recipe's recommended baking temperature by 25°F (5°C).

Sweet Shortcrust Pastry
PÂTE SABLÉE

With a texture that is more crumbly and richer than the pâte brisée sucrée, this crust is also used for sweet tarts, including classic desserts such as strawberry and lemon tarts, especially mini tarts.

WEIGHT about 15 ounces (425 g)

TART PAN SIZE 11 inches (28 cm) or 4 inches (10 cm; if making 6 to 8 mini tarts)

RECIPE Mini Lemon Meringue Tarts (page 180)

1⅔ cups (200 g) all-purpose flour

½ cup (65 g) confectioners' sugar

⅓ cup (35 g) ground almonds

⅓ cup plus 1 tablespoon (100 g) unsalted butter, at room temperature, plus more for greasing

1 medium egg

———

See instructions below.

Instructions for Making All Shortcrust Pastries

1 In a large bowl or the bowl of a stand mixer, mix together the dry ingredients.

2a For recipes using butter, add the butter to the dry mixture and work it until you get a sandy texture. Add the liquid ingredients (such as egg or water) to the mixture and combine until you have a smooth dough.

2b For recipes using olive oil or yogurt, add the oil or yogurt, egg, and water to the dry ingredients and mix until you obtain a smooth dough.

3 Shape the dough into a ball, wrap it in plastic wrap, and refrigerate for 30 minutes, or overnight.

4 Preheat the oven to 350°F (180°C). Line an 11-inch (28 cm) tart pan with parchment paper or grease it with unsalted butter.

5 After chilling, place the dough ball on a lightly floured surface and roll it out using a rolling pin into a circle that is 2 inches (5 cm) larger in diameter than the tart pan. Using a rolling pin or a sharp knife, trim off any excess dough from the edges. (To use your rolling pin, roll it from side to side over the dough, pressing lightly to cut the dough.) Prick the base with a fork.

6 Lay a sheet of parchment paper over the dough and fill it with pie weights, dried beans, or uncooked rice to prevent puffing during blind baking. (Blind baking is crucial to ensure the dough is cooked through in the center of the quiche.) Bake for 10 to 15 minutes, until the edges start to harden. (Note: The Yogurt Shortcrust Pastry needs less time to blind-bake, so keep an eye on it.)

7 After blind baking, add the filling of your choice, usually some ham, vegetables, cheese, or other ingredients, and pour over the *appareil à quiche*, which is a mixture of 4 eggs with 1 cup (240 ml) or more of heavy whipping cream and/or milk, depending on how rich the filling already is. Bake in the oven for 35 to 40 minutes until the filling is set and the crust is golden brown.

note The wrapped dough ball can be stored in the refrigerator for up to 2 days and in the freezer for up to 3 months. To save time if freezing, roll out the dough to form a circle either the size of your tart pan or a bit smaller. Wrap it well in plastic wrap and freeze flat. Before using, let it come to room temperature, then roll it out to the size needed and blind-bake it.

APPETIZERS
and STARTERS

Cheese and Green Asparagus Puff Pastry

FEUILLETÉS
AU FROMAGE ET ASPERGES VERTES

Here's a simple recipe to showcase green asparagus in a beautiful, flaky puff pastry.
These can be served as an appetizer or as a starter with a green salad.

YIELD 8 FEUILLETÉS
PREP TIME 10 MINUTES
COOK TIME 25 MINUTES

1 sheet frozen puff pastry
dough, thawed

32 thin green asparagus stalks,
trimmed

1 tablespoon olive oil

1 pinch salt

1 pinch black pepper

1½ cups (150 g) grated Swiss
cheese (such as Emmental
or Gruyère)

8 sprigs fresh lemon thyme
or regular thyme

1 egg yolk

1 Preheat the oven to 350°F (180°C) on the convection setting. Line a baking sheet with parchment paper.

2 Cut the puff pastry into 8 equal-size rectangles using a sharp knife and place on the prepared baking sheet.

3 Place the asparagus stalks in a large bowl with the oil, salt, and pepper and mix well to coat.

4 To assemble, position a puff pastry square like a diamond with a point on top and bottom. Sprinkle some of the grated cheese on the puff pastry, then lay 4 asparagus stalks vertically on the square and top with the leaves from a thyme sprig. Fold the sides of the puff pastry over the asparagus, overlapping them and pressing firmly to seal the edges. Repeat with the remaining puff pastry squares, cheese, asparagus, and thyme.

5 Add the egg yolk to a small bowl and dilute it with a few drops of cold water. Mix well with a fork to make an egg wash. Brush the visible parts of the puff pastry with the egg wash.

6 Bake for 25 to 30 minutes, until the crust is golden brown. Serve immediately.

Cheese Gougères

GOUGÈRES
AU FROMAGE

Cheese gougères are a classic of French cuisine. They are ideal as an appetizer, served with a glass of white wine or champagne.

1   Preheat the oven to 350°F (180°C) on the convection setting. Grease a baking sheet with butter or line with parchment paper.

2   Add 1 cup (240 ml) of water to a medium saucepan and bring to a boil. Once boiling, add the butter and salt. Remove the pan from the heat, then add all the flour at once (this is very important). Stir the mixture vigorously with a spatula or wooden spoon until the flour is fully incorporated and forms a thick lump. Return the pan to the stove and stir the dough continuously for 2 to 3 minutes over low heat; this will help the dough to dry. The dough is ready when it no longer sticks to the sides of the pan or the spatula. Remove the pan from the heat and let the dough cool slightly, then incorporate the eggs, one at a time, until well combined (you can use a spatula, wooden spoon, or hand mixer on low speed to mix). Add 1½ cups (150 g) of the cheese and the nutmeg and stir well.

3   Using two teaspoons or a piping bag with a medium-size tip or the tip cut, place small heaps of the dough on the prepared baking sheet. Sprinkle the gougères with the remaining ½ cup (50 g) cheese.

4   Bake for 20 to 25 minutes, until the gougères have doubled in size and start turning golden brown. Check the oven occasionally but without opening the door to prevent the gougères from falling. Transfer to a cooling rack and let cool for a bit. Serve warm.

note   For a lighter, airier texture, use ⅔ cup (80 g) of flour and ½ cup (65 g) of cornstarch. For a gluten-free option, use only 1 cup of cornstarch (130 g) or potato starch (165 g).

YIELD ABOUT 30 GOUGÈRES
PREP TIME 10 MINUTES
COOK TIME 30 MINUTES

⅓ cup (80 g) unsalted butter, at room temperature and cut into pieces, plus more for greasing

¼ teaspoon salt

1¼ cups (150 g) all-purpose flour (see Note)

4 medium eggs

2 cups (200 g) grated Gruyère cheese, divided

1 pinch ground nutmeg

TAPENADES D'ÉTÉ

When I have friends over, I like to prepare all variations: the classic with black olives, a milder one with green olives, and a tangy version with sun-dried tomatoes.

YIELD 8 TO 10 SERVINGS
PREP TIME 20 MINUTES

GREEN OLIVE TAPENADE WITH BASIL

1¼ cups (150 g) pitted green olives

5 anchovy fillets in oil (see Notes), drained

¼ cup (10 g) roughly chopped fresh basil

¼ cup (25 g) ground almonds

1 clove garlic

¼ cup (60 ml) olive oil

2 tablespoons fresh lemon juice

1 teaspoon honey (optional)

Black pepper

RED TAPENADE WITH SUN-DRIED TOMATOES AND WALNUTS

1 cup (120 g) sun-dried tomatoes in oil, drained

½ cup (60 g) pitted green olives

¼ cup (25 g) walnuts

5 anchovy fillets in oil (see Notes), drained

1 clove garlic

¼ cup (60 ml) olive oil

2 tablespoons fresh lemon juice

1 teaspoon honey (optional)

Black pepper

BLACK OLIVE TAPENADE

1¼ cups (150 g) pitted black olives

5 anchovy fillets in oil (see Notes), drained

2 teaspoons capers, drained

1 teaspoon Herbes de Provence (page 11)

1 clove garlic

¼ cup (60 ml) olive oil

2 tablespoons fresh lemon juice

Black pepper

FOR SERVING

Toasted baguette slices and/or crackers of choice

1 To make each tapenade, place all the ingredients of each one in a blender or a food processor and blend until smooth (see Notes).

2 Serve at room temperature (see Notes) as dips with toasted baguette slices and/or crackers.

———

notes

You can replace the anchovies with a pinch of sea salt.

If you are making all three tapenades, you don't need to clean your blender or food processor in between. Start with green, followed by red, and finish with black.

You can eat these dips straight away, or let the flavors infuse at room temperature for 1 to 2 hours. They will keep in an airtight container in the refrigerator for up to 1 week.

PANISSES
ET SAUCE MAYONNAISE ÉPICÉE

This is a forgotten classic of Provençal cuisine that deserves to be better known. These chickpea fries are naturally vegan, gluten-free, and dairy-free. Enjoy them as a side or a main dish with a salad.

1 **TO MAKE THE PANISSES:** Grease a rectangular glass baking dish, approximately 12 x 6 inches (30 x 15 cm), with oil.

2 Add 2 cups plus 2 tablespoons (500 ml) of the cold water, along with the salt and 1 tablespoon oil, to a medium saucepan and bring to a boil. Meanwhile, pour the chickpea flour into a large bowl. Gradually pour in the remaining 2 cups plus 2 tablespoons (500 ml) cold water while continuously stirring with a whisk or a wooden spoon to avoid lumps.

3 Pour the boiling water into the bowl with the flour while whisking until well combined. Transfer the mixture to the same saucepan and cook over medium-low heat for about 10 minutes, continuously stirring, until thickened and smooth. Immediately pour the mixture into the prepared dish, working fast to avoid it setting. Cover the dish with plastic wrap and refrigerate for at least 2 hours. Remove the hardened preparation from the dish. Slice into 3 x ½-inch (7.5 x 1.5 cm) french fries.

4 **TO MAKE THE SPICY TOMATO MAYONNAISE:** In a small bowl, mix all the mayonnaise ingredients until well combined. Refrigerate until ready to serve.

5 When ready to serve, cover the entire base of a large skillet with oil and heat over medium-high heat. Once hot, add the chickpea fries, working in batches to avoid overcrowding the pan, and cook for 2 to 3 minutes per side, until crispy and browned. Transfer to a paper towel–lined plate.

6 Transfer to a plate and sprinkle with black pepper, fleur de sel, and chopped parsley. Serve with the mayonnaise.

YIELD 6 TO 8 SERVINGS
PREP TIME 15 MINUTES, PLUS 2 HOURS CHILLING
COOK TIME 10 MINUTES

PANISSES

1 tablespoon olive oil, plus more for greasing and frying

4¼ cups (1 L) cold water, divided

¼ teaspoon salt

2½ cups (250 g) chickpea flour, sifted

SPICY TOMATO MAYONNAISE

½ cup (120 ml) Homemade Mayonnaise (page 12)

1 tablespoon tomato paste

1 tablespoon fresh lemon juice

⅛ teaspoon Espelette pepper (or use less cayenne pepper)

¼ teaspoon smoked paprika

1 pinch fleur de sel or sea salt flakes

FOR GARNISHING

Black pepper

Fleur de sel or sea salt flakes

Finely chopped fresh flat-leaf parsley

RILLETTES DE MAQUEREAU
AU CITRON ET AUX ARTICHAUTS

This mackerel rillettes is super simple to make and ideal to serve as an appetizer on toasted baguette slices. The combination of lemon and artichoke hearts goes perfectly with the smoked mackerel.

YIELD 8 SERVINGS
PREP TIME 15 MINUTES

1 whole smoked mackerel or
2 boneless, skinless fillets in oil,
drained

3 or 4 canned or jarred
artichoke hearts,
in brine or oil, drained
and finely chopped

2 tablespoons
finely chopped chives

1 large lemon, for zesting
and juicing

Salt and black pepper

3 tablespoons olive oil

Toasted baguette slices,
for serving

1 If you are using a whole smoked mackerel, remove the skin, head, and bones, leaving only the fillets. If you are using boneless, skinless fillets, check to make sure there are no bones or skin left.

2 In a large bowl, flake the mackerel flesh with a fork. Add the chopped artichokes and chives to the bowl. Grate in the zest of the whole lemon, then cut the lemon in half and squeeze in 1 to 2 tablespoons of juice, or to taste. Season with a pinch each of salt and pepper, drizzle with the oil, and mix well. Taste and adjust the seasoning by adding a little more salt and/or lemon juice if needed.

3 Serve with toasted baguette slices.

———

note The mackerel rillettes will keep in an airtight container in the refrigerator for 2 to 3 days. Remove from the fridge 30 minutes before serving to allow the flavors to develop.

PETITS CANAPÉS
RAPIDES ET FACILES

Canapés are small appetizers served on slices of bread or baguette as an appetizer. In France, we like to serve them when we have guests over. Here are three easy-to-prepare versions that are sure to please everyone.

1 Lightly toast all 18 slices of baguette using your preferred method for toasting bread.

2 **TO MAKE THE SALAMI AND PICKLE CANAPÉS:** Spread 6 slices of the toasted baguette each with 1 teaspoon of butter. Top each toast with a parsley leaf, a slice of salami, and a piece of pickle. Finish each one with a sprinkle of pepper.

3 **TO MAKE THE SMOKED SALMON CANAPÉS:** Spread 6 slices of the toasted baguette each with 2 teaspoons of cream cheese. Top each toast with a cucumber slice, a piece of smoked salmon, and some dill. Finish each one with some grated lemon zest and a sprinkle of pepper.

4 **TO MAKE THE VEGETARIAN CANAPÉS:** Spread the remaining 6 slices of toasted baguette each with 2 teaspoons of black olive tapenade. Top with a basil leaf and a cherry tomato half, cut side up. Finish each one with a sprinkle of pepper.

5 You can add a toothpick to help hold each canapé together. Serve immediately.

———

notes

If you want to prepare these canapés in advance, do so no more than 1 hour before serving them; otherwise, the baguette will lose its crispness.

You can vary and experiment with the canapé toppings depending on the ingredients you have on hand.

YIELD 18 CANAPÉS
PREP TIME 10 MINUTES

SALAMI AND PICKLE CANAPÉS

6 slices (½ inch, or 6 mm, thick) baguette

2 tablespoons salted butter

6 flat-leaf parsley leaves

6 slices salami

3 pickles, cut in half

Black pepper

SMOKED SALMON CANAPÉS

6 slices (½ inch, or 6 mm, thick) baguette

¼ cup (60 g) cream cheese

6 thin slices cucumber

3½ ounces (100 g) smoked salmon, cut into 6 equal-size pieces

2 sprigs fresh dill

1 lemon, for zesting

Black pepper

VEGETARIAN CANAPÉS

6 slices (½ inch, or 6 mm, thick) baguette

¼ cup (40 g) Black Olive Tapenade (page 22)

6 leaves fresh basil

3 cherry tomatoes, cut in half

Black pepper

Whipped Brie with Honey, Blackberries, and Walnuts

BRIE FOUETTÉ
AU MIEL, MÛRES ET AUX NOIX

This recipe for whipped Brie is simple, elegant, and perfect for any occasion. I like to serve it as an appetizer or have it accompany a meal. It never lasts long either way it's served!

YIELD 8 TO 10 SERVINGS
PREP TIME 15 MINUTES, PLUS 30 MINUTES RESTING
COOK TIME 5 MINUTES

14 ounces (400 g) chilled Brie cheese (see Note)

½ cup (75 g) fresh blackberries

1 tablespoon honey, plus more for drizzling

⅓ cup (35 g) whole walnuts

2 sprigs fresh rosemary

Fleur de sel or sea salt flakes

Black pepper

Toasted baguette slices, for serving

1 While the Brie is still cold and hard, use a sharp knife to remove the rind, then let the cheese rest at room temperature for 30 minutes to soften.

2 Place the Brie in the bowl of a stand mixer with a paddle attachment. Beat on medium speed for 5 to 10 minutes, until creamy.

3 Meanwhile, place the blackberries in a small bowl with the 1 tablespoon honey. Microwave for 30 to 45 seconds on medium power to slightly soften them.

4 Place the walnuts in a dry skillet (without any oil) and toast over medium heat until the walnuts start to turn darker in color, stirring regularly, about 5 minutes. Set aside and let cool a little, then roughly chop them.

5 Spread the whipped Brie on a serving plate and garnish with the blackberries, toasted walnuts, and rosemary sprigs. Finish with a drizzle of honey and sprinkle with fleur de sel,and pepper and serve with toasted baguette slices.

———

note This recipe is also great with other soft cheeses, such as Camembert and Époisses.

Sardine Toasts with Marinated Red Pepper and Basil

TOASTS DE SARDINES
AU POIVRON ROUGE MARINÉ ET AU BASILIC

I always make sure to have a tin of sardines in my pantry. They have a long shelf life and are versatile, making them ideal either for a quick, simple snack on bread with salted butter or, as in this recipe, a fancy appetizer.

1 **TO MAKE THE MARINATED RED PEPPERS:** Preheat the oven on the broiler setting.

2 Place the red peppers on a baking sheet, cut sides down, and broil for 15 to 20 minutes, until they start to blacken. Remove the peppers from the oven and immediately wrap them in plastic wrap, sealing it tightly. Let cool for 10 minutes. The condensation will help loosen the skin.

3 Peel the peppers, then cut them into large strips. Season with the fleur de sel. If you plan on eating all the bell peppers right away, place them in a medium bowl with the oil and let them marinate for 30 minutes. If you are preparing them in advance or want to save leftovers, place them in an airtight container, making sure the peppers are fully covered with oil (adding more if needed) and refrigerate for up to 5 days.

4 **MEANWHILE, MAKE THE SARDINE TOASTS:** Toast the bread using your preferred method for toasting bread. Rub the garlic clove over both sides of the toasted bread.

5 Open the sardines lengthwise, delicately removing the central bone. Arrange a few strips of marinated red pepper on each toast, then place a sardine half on top. Finish each toast with basil leaves, red onion slices, and a pinch each of fleur de sel and Espelette pepper. Serve immediately.

---

note For a quicker version, replace the marinated red peppers with fresh tomatoes slices seasoned with fleur de sel and a drizzle of olive oil.

YIELD 8 TOASTS
PREP TIME 10 MINUTES, PLUS 30 MINUTES MARINATING
COOK TIME 20 MINUTES

MARINATED RED PEPPERS
2 medium red bell peppers (see Note), cut in half and seeds removed

1 pinch fleur de sel or sea salt flakes

¼ cup (60 ml) olive oil

SARDINE TOASTS
4 slices country bread, cut in half

1 clove garlic, peeled

4 sardines in oil, drained

½ cup (20 g) fresh basil leaves

½ small red onion, thinly sliced

Fleur de sel or sea salt flakes

Espelette or cayenne pepper

CAKE SALÉ
AU BROCOLI, YAOURT ET CIBOULETTE

In France, we love cakes salés, which are savory loaf cakes that you can make with whatever vegetables you have on hand. I love this version with broccoli and chives—it is as beautiful as it is tasty.

YIELD 6 SERVINGS
PREP TIME 20 MINUTES
COOK TIME 50 MINUTES

¼ cup (60 ml) olive oil, plus more for greasing

½ head broccoli (about 6 ounces, or 170 g) trimmed and separated into 7 or 8 florets

1¼ cups (150 g) all-purpose flour

⅓ cup (50 g) cornstarch

2 teaspoons baking powder

1 teaspoon ground turmeric

1½ teaspoons salt

Black pepper

3 large eggs

⅔ cup (160 g) plain yogurt (3.5% fat)

¼ cup (11 g) finely chopped chives

2 tablespoons fresh lemon juice

1 Preheat the oven to 350°F (180°C) on the convection setting. Grease an 8½ x 4½-inch (21 x 11 cm) metal loaf pan with oil.

2 Bring a large pot of water to a boil. Meanwhile, prepare a large bowl with cold water and ice for an ice bath.

3 Add the broccoli florets to the boiling water and blanch for 2 minutes. Remove the pot from the heat and drain. Immediately rinse the broccoli under cold running water, then place the florets in the ice bath for 2 minutes to preserve their bright-green color. Drain well.

4 In a large bowl, mix the flour, cornstarch, baking powder, turmeric, salt, and pepper to taste until well combined. Mix in the eggs, one at a time, followed by the yogurt and oil. Finally, fold in the chives and lemon juice.

5 Pour the cake mixture into the prepared loaf pan, then press the broccoli florets into the cake batter.

6 Bake for 45 to 50 minutes, until a knife inserted in the center comes out clean. If the cake starts to turn dark, cover with aluminum foil or parchment paper while baking. Let cool for 5 minutes before removing from the pan, then let cool to room temperature before slicing and serving.

———

note You can serve this cake salé as a starter for brunch or lunch with a green salad and soup, such as the Roasted Tomato and Bell Pepper Soup (page 51). For a quick lunch, serve it as a main with a green salad and the Creamy Chive Dip (page 143).

Roasted Leeks with Lemon-Dill Vinaigrette

POIREAUX RÔTIS
À LA VINAIGRETTE À L'ANETH ET CITRON

Leeks in vinaigrette are a classic French starter. The leeks are usually steamed or boiled, but I prefer to roast them in the oven, which gives them a delicious, caramelized note. The lemon-dill vinaigrette adds freshness, and don't forget the bread crumbs for some crunch.

1 **TO MAKE THE ROASTED LEEKS:** Preheat the oven to 350°F (180°C) on the convection setting. Line a baking sheet with parchment paper.

2 Remove and discard the outer green layers of the leeks. Cut the leeks in half lengthwise and wash thoroughly between the layers to remove any dirt. Cut each half crosswise into 2 or 3 pieces. Brush the leeks with the 2 tablespoons oil, season with salt and pepper, and sprinkle with the Espelette pepper. Place them on the prepared baking sheet, cut sides down.

3 Bake for 20 to 25 minutes, until a toothpick inserted into them goes in easily (cook time will depend on the size of the leeks).

4 **MEANWHILE, MAKE THE LEMON-DILL VINAIGRETTE:** In a small bowl, combine the mustard, honey, 2 tablespoons lemon juice, and fleur de sel. Gradually add the ¼ cup (60 ml) oil while whisking until well combined. Finish by mixing in the shallot, dill, grated lemon zest (reserving a little for garnishing), and pepper.

5 **TO MAKE THE CRISPY BREAD CRUMBS:** In a small bowl, combine the bread crumbs and 1 tablespoon oil. Heat a medium pan or skillet over medium heat. Add the bread crumbs and toast, stirring regularly, until they are golden brown.

6 Place the roasted leeks on a plate, drizzle the vinaigrette over them, and top with the crispy bread crumbs and more lemon zest. Serve warm, lukewarm, or cold.

YIELD 4 SERVINGS
PREP TIME 10 MINUTES
COOK TIME 25 MINUTES

ROASTED LEEKS

4 large leeks

2 tablespoons olive oil

Salt and black pepper

1 teaspoon Espelette pepper

LEMON-DILL VINAIGRETTE

1 tablespoon whole grain Dijon mustard

1 teaspoon honey or agave syrup

1 medium lemon, for zesting and juicing, divided

1 pinch fleur de sel or sea salt flakes

¼ cup (60 ml) olive oil

1 small shallot, minced

½ cup (25 g) chopped fresh dill

Black pepper

CRISPY BREAD CRUMBS

½ cup panko (40 g) or regular (50 g) bread crumbs

1 tablespoon olive oil

Baked Eggs with Sun-Dried Tomatoes and Spinach

ŒUFS COCOTTE
TOMATES SÉCHÉES ET ÉPINARDS

Œufs cocotte are a traditional French way to prepare eggs. They are usually served as a starter with mouillettes, small toasted breadsticks that you dip in the runny egg yolk. I also like to serve these for brunch.

YIELD 4 SERVINGS
PREP TIME 5 MINUTES
COOK TIME 15 MINUTES

1 tablespoon olive oil

1 clove garlic, minced

4 cups (120 g) baby spinach

Salt and black pepper

½ cup (120 ml) heavy whipping cream

8 sun-dried tomatoes in oil, drained and roughly chopped

4 medium eggs

1 handful fresh basil leaves

8 slices toasted bread, cut into sticks, for serving

1 Preheat the oven at 350 °F (180°C) on the convection setting. Place four 3½-inch (9 cm) ramekins in the oven for 3 to 5 minutes while the oven is heating. Bring a kettle or pot of water to a boil.

2 Meanwhile, heat the oil in a small pan over medium heat. Add the garlic and sauté for 30 seconds, or until fragrant. Add the spinach and sauté for a couple minutes, or until just wilted. Season with salt and pepper and remove the pan from the heat.

3 Carefully transfer the 4 warm ramekins to a baking dish and fill the dish three-quarters with the boiling water to create a water bath (bain-marie).

4 Pour 2 tablespoons of cream into each ramekin, then add spinach and sun-dried tomato pieces to each dish. Season with salt and pepper. Crack an egg into each ramekin and season with a little pepper.

5 Carefully place the baking dish in the oven and bake for 10 to 15 minutes, until the egg whites are soft and silky and the yolks are slightly runny and velvety. Remove the ramekins from the pan and place each one on a small plate. Garnish with basil leaves and serve with the toasted breadsticks.

———

note You can customize this recipe to your taste by adding grated cheese, sautéed mushrooms, ham, and so on to your œuf cocottes.

Whipped Brown Butter with Espelette Pepper

BEURRE NOISETTE FOUETTÉ
AU PIMENT D'ESPELETTE

Here is a quick and easy recipe that is perfect for impressing your guests at a dinner party. Brown butter has a unique and delicious flavor, and when combined with Espelette pepper, it adds an irresistible spicy touch. The whipped texture of this butter is incredible—airy and so pleasant. Place this dish in the center of the table as an appetizer or during the meal, and it will be gone in no time!

1 Prepare a large bowl filled with cold water and ice cubes for an ice bath. Place a medium stainless steel bowl on top of the ice bath; this will be used to whip the butter.

2 Place the butter in a medium skillet over medium heat. Once it starts bubbling, continue cooking it, stirring regularly, until the butter forms small light-brown particles and emits a nutty aroma, 5 to 8 minutes. (Be careful not to overcook your butter; i.e., if you start to see dark-brown-to-black particles, stop cooking immediately.)

3 Pour the brown butter into the stainless steel bowl placed over the ice bath. Whip the butter by hand until it cools down and turns a beige color. Add the fleur de sel and Espelette pepper and whip until incorporated. Stop whipping once the butter is well mixed and airy.

4 Serve immediately with bread slices.

------

note Store this whipped butter in an airtight container in the refrigerator for up to 2 weeks. Remove the butter from the refrigerator about 30 minutes before serving to let it soften to a spreadable consistency.

YIELD 4 TO 8 SERVINGS
PREP TIME 5 MINUTES
COOK TIME 8 MINUTES

½ cup (120 g) unsalted butter, at room temperature and cut into pieces

½ teaspoon fleur de sel or sea salt

1 pinch Espelette pepper (or use less cayenne pepper), or to taste

Sourdough bread or baguette slices, for serving

SOUPS

Chilled Zucchini and Pea Soup

SOUPE FROIDE
DE COURGETTES ET PETITS POIS

This is a healthy, refreshing soup that I love to serve in summer, either as a main course with toasted bread, as a starter, or an appetizer in small glasses.

YIELD 4 SERVINGS
PREP TIME 10 MINUTES
COOK TIME 10 MINUTES

Salt

2 medium zucchini (14 ounces, or 400 g), cut into ½-inch-thick (1.5 cm) slices

2 cloves garlic, peeled

2 cups (270 g) frozen peas

¼ cup (10 g) fresh basil leaves, plus more for garnishing

¼ cup (13 g) fresh mint leaves, plus more for garnishing

¼ cup (13 g) roughly chopped flat-leaf parsley

⅔ cup (150 g) cream cheese

3 to 4 tablespoons fresh lime juice (about 1 lime), or to taste

Black pepper

1 cup (240 ml) cold water

4 small ice cubes

Olive oil, for drizzling

1 Bring a large pot of salted water to a boil.

2 Add the zucchini and garlic cloves and cook for 10 to 12 minutes, until the zucchini are fork-tender. Add the frozen peas 5 minutes before the end of cooking. Drain and rinse the vegetables under cold water to cool.

3 Transfer the cooked zucchini, garlic cloves, and peas to a blender along with the basil, mint, parsley, cream cheese, and lime juice. Season with salt and pepper. Add the cold water and ice cubes and blend until smooth.

4 Serve immediately, or place in the refrigerator to chill longer. Ladle the soup into bowls, garnish with basil and mint leaves, and drizzle with oil.

———

note On colder days, you can serve this soup hot. Simply omit the ice cubes in step 3, then transfer the blended soup to a pot and heat over low heat for a couple minutes, or until warmed through.

Creamy Mushroom and Thyme Soup

VELOUTÉ DE CHAMPIGNONS
AU THYM

This creamy mushroom soup is a classic of French cuisine that I love to serve for a quick dinner in the autumn or as a starter for a festive meal.

1 In a large skillet, heat the oil over medium-high heat. Add the onion, shallot, and garlic and cook until they turn translucent.

2 Add the sliced mushrooms, season with salt and pepper, and sauté over medium-high heat for 15 minutes, or until the mushrooms are dark brown on both sides. Toward the end of cooking, add the butter to enhance the mushrooms' flavor and sauté for another 2 minutes. Set aside some mushroom slices for garnish.

3 Add the flour to the pan and stir until well combined. Gradually pour in the milk, stirring constantly until the flour is fully incorporated and no lumps remain. Pour in the broth and add the bay leaves, thyme sprigs, and lemon juice. Let simmer for 15 minutes.

4 Remove and discard the bay leaves and thyme sprigs, then transfer the soup to a blender (be careful transferring the hot soup to the blender, which you may need to do in batches). Blend on high speed until smooth and creamy. (If the consistency is too thick, add some water to reach the desired texture.)

5 Ladle the soup into bowls and garnish with thyme leaves, the reserved mushroom slices, and a dollop of crème fraîche.

YIELD 2 TO 4 SERVINGS
PREP TIME 15 MINUTES
COOK TIME 30 MINUTES

2 tablespoons olive oil

1 small yellow onion, finely chopped

1 small shallot, finely chopped

3 cloves garlic, minced

1 pound (455 g) button mushrooms (see Note), thinly sliced

Salt and black pepper

1 tablespoon unsalted butter

2 tablespoons all-purpose flour

1½ cups (360 ml) whole milk

2½ cups (600 ml) vegetable broth

2 bay leaves

6 sprigs fresh thyme, plus more leaves for garnishing

2 tablespoons lemon juice

¼ cup (60 g) crème fraîche or sour cream, for garnishing

note You can make this soup with any type of mushroom or even a mix of different varieties.

Green Tortellini Soup with Pistou

SOUPE VERTE
DE TORTELLINI ET PISTOU

YIELD 3 OR 4 SERVINGS
PREP TIME 10 MINUTES
COOK TIME 30 MINUTES

TORTELLINI SOUP

2 tablespoons olive oil

1 medium yellow onion, thinly sliced

1 medium carrot, cut into ¼-inch (6 mm) dice

1 large zucchini, cut into ¼-inch (6 mm) dice

1 clove garlic, minced

Salt and black pepper

2 cups (480 ml) vegetable broth

6 sprigs fresh thyme

2 bay leaves

9 ounces (250 g) fresh tortellini, filled with spinach and ricotta

3 cups (90 g) baby spinach

1 cup fresh (145 g) or frozen (135 g) peas

½ medium lemon, for squeezing

PISTOU SAUCE

2 cups (40 g) fresh basil leaves

1 clove garlic, minced

½ cup (60 g) grated Parmesan cheese

3 tablespoons olive oil

1 tablespoon fresh lemon juice

1 pinch fleur de sel or sea salt

Taking inspiration from the traditional Provençal dish pistou soup, this green tortellini soup incorporates vibrant vegetables and a pistou sauce, which is akin to Italian pesto.

1 **TO MAKE THE TORTELLINI SOUP:** In a large pot, heat the 2 tablespoons oil over medium heat. Add the onion, carrot, zucchini, and garlic and sauté for 5 minutes. Season with salt and pepper.

2 Pour in the broth and 4 cups (960 ml) of water. Add the thyme sprigs and bay leaves and season with salt. Reduce the heat to medium-low and let simmer for 15 to 20 minutes, covered with the lid, until the vegetables are tender.

3 **MEANWHILE, MAKE THE PISTOU SAUCE:** Place all the sauce ingredients in a tall container and blend with an immersion blender until it forms a paste. (You can use a countertop blender or food processor, but the texture won't be ideal.)

4 Once the vegetables are cooked, add the tortellini, spinach, and peas to the pot and cook for about 5 minutes.

5 Just before serving, stir in 1 tablespoon of pistou sauce and a squeeze of lemon juice. Mix well. Ladle the soup into bowls and garnish with an extra spoonful of pistou sauce on top.

note To make this soup in advance, prepare it through step 2. You can also make the pistou sauce ahead of time. Store separately in airtight containers in the refrigerator for 2 to 3 days. Right before serving, reheat the soup starting at step 4, adding the tortellini, spinach, and peas, then continue with step 5.

Roasted Tomato and Bell Pepper Soup

SOUPE DE TOMATES
ET DE POIVRONS RÔTIS

This is one of my favorite recipes for a quick and tasty soup. I have included savory granola as a topping, which I love to serve with soups and salads.

1 **TO MAKE THE SAVORY GRANOLA:** Preheat the oven to 320°F (160°C) on the convection setting. Line a baking sheet with parchment paper.

2 In a large bowl, mix all the granola ingredients with a wooden spoon until well combined. Spread the granola mixture on the prepared baking sheet in a single layer. Bake for 20 to 25 minutes, until the granola has a nice light-brown color. Let cool completely before transferring to an airtight container. Store in a dry place away from light for up to 3 weeks.

3 **TO MAKE THE SOUP:** Preheat the oven to 350°F (180°C) on the convection setting.

4 Line a baking sheet with parchment paper and place the bell peppers, onion, tomatoes, and garlic cloves on it. Sprinkle the vegetables with the herbes de Provence and drizzle with the oil. Roast for 25 to 30 minutes, until the skins of the bell peppers start to blacken. Remove from the oven and peel the garlic cloves. Place the roasted vegetables and peeled garlic in a blender. Heat the broth in the microwave for 2 minutes on high power, then add it to the blender with the balsamic vinegar. Blend until smooth, adding more broth or water if needed. Season with salt and pepper.

5 Ladle the soup into bowls and garnish with the goat cheese and savory granola.

———

note This soup can also be served chilled during the summer months.

YIELD 2 SERVINGS
PREP TIME 10 MINUTES
COOK TIME 50 MINUTES

SAVORY GRANOLA

1½ cups (150 g) rolled oats

1 cup (140 g) mixed seeds of choice (I use equal amounts of pumpkin, sunflower, flax, and white sesame seeds)

1 large egg white

¼ cup (60 ml) olive oil

1 tablespoon honey

1 tablespoon Dijon mustard

½ teaspoon smoked paprika

Salt and black pepper

SOUP

2 red bell peppers (about 10 ounces, or 300 g), cut into quarters

1 medium red onion, cut into quarters

6 tomatoes (about 26 ounces, or 750 g), cut into quarters

2 cloves garlic, skins on

1 tablespoon Herbes de Provence (page 11)

3 tablespoons (45 ml) olive oil

1½ cups (360 ml) vegetable broth, plus more if needed (optional)

1 tablespoon balsamic vinegar

Salt and black pepper

⅓ cup (50 g) crumbled fresh goat or feta cheese, for garnishing

Fish Soup with Fennel and Orange

SOUPE DE POISSON
AU FENOUIL ET À L'ORANGE

For fish fans like me, here's a simple version of fish soup with salmon and cod and flavors of fennel and orange. Since this soup is easy to make, you can enjoy it as a healthy weekday meal or serve it when having guests over.

YIELD 4 SERVINGS
PREP TIME 15 MINUTES
COOK TIME 40 MINUTES

1 large fennel bulb

2 tablespoons olive oil

1 large yellow onion, finely chopped

1 large carrot, cut into ¼-inch (6 mm) dice

1 celery rib, cut into ¼-inch (6 mm) dice

3 cloves garlic, minced

Salt and black pepper

2 tablespoons tomato paste

¼ cup (60 ml) pastis or dry white wine

1 can (14 ounces, or 400 g) whole peeled tomatoes

5 cups (1.2 L) fish stock

1 large orange, for peeling and juicing

5 sprigs fresh thyme

2 bay leaves

1 pound (450 g) baby potatoes, cut into quarters

21 ounces (600 g) skinless fish fillets (you can use a mix of salmon and white fish, such as cod)

1 Remove the hard end of the fennel bulb and the fronds, reserving the fronds for garnishing. Thinly slice the fennel bulb.

2 In a large pot, heat the oil over medium heat. Add the onion, carrot, and celery and sauté for 2 minutes. Add the garlic and fennel slices and sauté for another minute. Season with salt and pepper.

3 Add the tomato paste and mix well. Pour in the pastis and deglaze the pot by scraping the bottom of the pot with a wooden spoon to release any browned bits. Add the whole tomatoes with their juices, the fish stock, orange peels, thyme, and bay leaves. Add the potatoes, reduce the heat to medium-low, and let simmer for about 30 minutes, or until the potatoes are fork-tender.

4 Meanwhile, season the fish fillets with salt and pepper, then cut the fillets into large cubes.

5 Once the potatoes are tender, add the fish pieces to the soup and cook for a few minutes until they turn opaque, about 5 minutes.

6 Ladle into bowls, drizzle with orange juice, and garnish with the reserved fennel fronds.

———

note To make this soup a day in advance, prepare it up to step 3, then refrigerate it. When ready to serve, continue at step 4, and the soup will be ready in 10 minutes.

Rustic Vegetable Soup

POTAGE DE LÉGUMES

This vegetable soup is one of my winter staples. It's the perfect recipe to make when you need to use up vegetables. And just as my grandmother would, I like to serve this soup with homemade croutons made with stale bread.

1 **TO MAKE THE SOUP:** In a large saucepan, melt the butter over medium heat. Add the onion, carrots, leeks, and celery and sauté for 3 minutes. Season with salt and pepper and add the cloves. Pour in the broth and add the potatoes and bay leaves. Bring to a boil, then reduce the heat to medium-low and let cook for 25 to 30 minutes, until all the vegetables are fork-tender.

2 **MEANWHILE, MAKE THE CROUTONS:** Preheat the oven to 390°F (200°C) on the convection setting. Line a baking sheet with parchment paper.

3 Place the bread cubes in a large bowl. Add the oil and pinch of salt and, using your hands, mix well to coat evenly; this will prevent the croutons from blackening in the oven. Transfer to the prepared baking sheet, spacing them well apart. Bake for 8 to 10 minutes, until golden brown.

4 When the vegetables are fork-tender, remove and discard the bay leaves. Using an immersion or countertop blender (be careful transferring the hot soup to a countertop blender, which you may need to do in batches), blend until smooth. (If the soup is too thick, add a little water and blend again.)

5 Ladle the soup into bowls and garnish each bowl with a dollop of crème fraîche, some croutons, and chopped parsley.

note You can freeze this soup for up to 3 months in an airtight container. To thaw, place it in the refrigerator several hours before serving, then reheat over medium heat before serving.

YIELD 4 SERVINGS
PREP TIME 10 MINUTES
COOK TIME 30 MINUTES

SOUP

2 tablespoons unsalted butter

1 medium yellow onion, cut into quarters

2 medium carrots (about 10 ounces, or 300 g), peeled and cut into slices

2 large leeks (about 14 ounces, or 400 g), cut into slices from the white to light green parts

2 celery ribs (about 3½ ounces, or 100 g), roughly chopped

Salt and black pepper

1 pinch ground cloves

5½ cups (1.3 L) vegetable broth

4 starchy potatoes (1 pound, or 455 g), peeled and cut into 1-inch (2.5 cm) cubes

2 bay leaves

CROUTONS

¼ baguette or crusty bread (3 to 4 ounces, or 85 to 115 g), cut into ½-inch (1.5 cm) cubes

¼ cup (60 ml) olive oil

1 pinch salt

FOR GARNISHING

¼ cup (60 g) crème fraîche or sour cream

½ cup (18 g) finely chopped fresh curly parsley

SALADS

Endive Salad with Orange, Cheese, and Walnuts

SALADE D'ENDIVES
À L'ORANGE, AU FROMAGE ET AUX NOIX

This is one of my favorite winter salads. The bitterness of the endives is perfectly balanced by the sweetness and delicate acidity of the oranges, while the walnuts add a delicious crunch. And don't forget the cheese for extra flavor!

YIELD 4 SERVINGS
PREP TIME 15 MINUTES

HONEY–ORANGE JUICE VINAIGRETTE

2 teaspoons Dijon mustard

1 teaspoon honey

2 tablespoons apple cider vinegar

3 tablespoons fresh orange juice

1 generous pinch fleur de sel or sea salt flakes

¼ cup (60 ml) walnut or olive oil

SALAD

4 endives (white and red), cut into slices, reserving a few whole leaves for garnishing

3½ ounces (100 g) Mimolette cheese (see Note), cut into ½-inch (1.5 cm) cubes

2 oranges, peeled and cut into slices

1 cup (100 g) whole walnuts

1 **TO MAKE THE HONEY–ORANGE JUICE VINAIGRETTE:** In a small bowl, combine the mustard, honey, vinegar, orange juice, and sea salt. Slowly add the oil while whisking until well combined.

2 **TO MAKE THE SALAD:** In a large salad bowl, combine the endive slices and cheese. Add half of the vinaigrette and mix well.

3 Transfer the salad to a serving plate, arrange the orange slices and reserved endive leaves on top, and sprinkle with the walnuts.

4 Drizzle the remaining vinaigrette over the salad. Serve immediately.

———

note This recipe is traditionally made with Mimolette, a French cheese from northern France that is famous for its orange color. If you can't find Mimolette, the best and, in my opinion, most delicious alternative is Cheddar cheese.

Warm Goat Cheese and Strawberry Salad

SALADE DE CHÈVRE CHAUD
ET DE FRAISES

Warm goat cheese salad has always been a favorite bistro dish of mine. Here, I've added a delightful twist by pairing the creamy goat cheese with a strawberry vinaigrette and fresh strawberries.

1 **TO MAKE THE SALAD:** Preheat the oven to 390°F (200°C) on the convection setting.

2 Line a baking sheet with parchment paper, then arrange the baguette slices on it. Drizzle the 2 tablespoons oil over the bread slices. Top each bread slice with a slice of goat cheese, some thyme leaves, and a pinch each of salt and pepper. Bake for 10 to 15 minutes, until the goat cheese begins to melt.

3 Place the walnuts in a dry skillet (without any oil) and toast over medium heat until the walnuts start to turn darker in color, stirring regularly, about 5 minutes. Set aside and let cool a little, then roughly chop them.

4 **TO MAKE THE VINAIGRETTE:** In a small bowl, mash the 3 strawberries with a fork. Add the vinegar and season with salt and a few twists of freshly ground pepper. Gradually pour in the ¼ cup (60 ml) oil while whisking until well combined.

5 Add the salad greens, strawberry halves, cherry tomatoes, and toasted walnuts to a medium salad bowl and toss with half of the vinaigrette. Divide the salad between plates, top with the warm goat-cheese toasts, and drizzle with the remaining vinaigrette. Serve immediately.

note You can replace the strawberries in the salad and vinaigrette with raspberries, blackberries, or figs.

YIELD 2 SERVINGS
PREP TIME 10 MINUTES
COOK TIME 15 MINUTES

SALAD

8 slices (½ inch, or 1.5 cm, thick) baguette

2 tablespoons olive oil

1 log (4 ounces, or 113 g) fresh goat cheese, cut into 8 slices

4 sprigs fresh thyme

Salt and black pepper

½ cup (50 g) whole walnuts

5 cups (175 g) mixed salad greens

7 ounces (200 g) strawberries (see Note), cut in half

½ cup (50 g) cherry tomatoes, cut in half

STRAWBERRY VINAIGRETTE

3 strawberries (see Note)

2 tablespoons white wine vinegar

Salt and black pepper

¼ cup (60 ml) olive oil

SALADE DE CROÛTONS ET DE TOMATES
À LA VINAIGRETTE DE CITRON ET D'ANCHOIS

This salad is inspired by the famous Italian panzanella but with a French twist. I like to serve it in summer as a side dish for barbecues or as a main course for a quick lunch.

YIELD 4 SERVINGS
PREP TIME 10 MINUTES
COOK TIME 10 MINUTES

CROUTONS

4 slices country bread, cut into 1- to 1½-inch (2.5 to 4 cm) cubes

3 tablespoons olive oil

Salt

LEMON-ANCHOVY VINAIGRETTE

1 teaspoon Dijon mustard

1 teaspoon honey

2 anchovy fillets in oil, drained and finely chopped

2 tablespoons fresh lemon juice

½ clove garlic, finely chopped

Salt and black pepper

¼ cup (60 ml) olive oil

SALAD

2 pounds (900 g) tomatoes, cut into quarters or sixths depending on their size

1 medium red onion, thinly sliced

3 tablespoons capers, drained

⅓ cup (12 g) chopped fresh curly parsley

6 anchovy fillets, roughly chopped

1 **TO MAKE THE CROUTONS:** Preheat the oven to 390°F (200°C) on the convection setting. Line a baking sheet with parchment paper

2 In a large salad bowl, combine the bread cubes with the 3 tablespoons oil and salt to taste. Using your hands, mix well to coat evenly; this will prevent the croutons from blackening in the oven. Transfer the bread cubes to the prepared baking sheet, spacing them well apart. Bake for 8 to 10 minutes, until golden brown. Let cool.

3 **MEANWHILE, MAKE THE LEMON-ANCHOVY VINAIGRETTE:** In a small bowl, combine the mustard, honey, 2 anchovies, lemon juice, garlic, and a pinch each of salt and pepper. Gradually add the ¼ cup (60 ml) oil while whisking until well combined.

4 **TO MAKE THE SALAD:** Add the tomatoes, onion, capers, parsley, 6 anchovies, and croutons to the bowl the bread cubes were mixed in and toss with all the vinaigrette. Let sit for 5 to 10 minutes to allow the flavors to meld and the croutons to soften a little. Serve immediately.

note The croutons will become soggy rather quickly. If you want to make this salad in advance, you can prepare all the parts (croutons, vinaigrette, and salad) and refrigerate the vinaigrette and salad separately until right before serving, then assemble and let sit for 10 minutes to infuse the flavors.

Pea Salad with Mint and Smoked Salmon

SALADE DE PETITS POIS
À LA MENTHE ET AU SAUMON FUMÉ

This salad is very quick to prepare, making it one of my favorite choices for a quick lunch. The delicate sweetness of the peas blends perfectly with the refreshing mint and tasty smoked salmon.

1   Bring a large pot of water to a boil. Prepare a bowl of cold water with ice cubes for an ice bath.

2   Cook the peas in the boiling water for 5 to 10 minutes if fresh or 3 minutes if frozen, until crisp-tender. Drain, rinse under cold water, and then place in the ice bath for 2 minutes. Drain again.

3   In a large salad bowl, combine the peas, cucumber, arugula, mint, and dill. Crumble the smoked salmon and add it to the bowl. Grate the lemon zest over the salad.

4   Right before serving, add 2 tablespoons lemon juice, oil, fleur de sel, and pepper to taste and mix well. Transfer to a serving plate. Serve immediately.

―――――

notes   If you can't find hot-smoked salmon, place a skinless salmon fillet in a small oven-safe dish, season it with salt and pepper, and drizzle it with olive oil. Bake in an oven preheated to 390°F (200°C) for 20 minutes, or until the flesh is pale pink and flakes easily with a fork. Let cool, then flake with a fork.

For a quicker version, replace the hot-smoked salmon with 2 slices of smoked salmon cut into 1-inch (2.5 cm) pieces.

YIELD 2 OR 3 SERVINGS
PREP TIME 10 MINUTES
COOK TIME 5 MINUTES

2 cups fresh (290 g) or frozen (270 g) peas

½ English cucumber, cut in half lengthwise, then thinly sliced into half-moons

1 cup (20 g) arugula

½ cup (25 g) roughly chopped fresh mint, plus more leaves for garnishing

½ cup (25 g) roughly chopped fresh dill, plus more for garnishing

1 hot-smoked salmon fillet (7 ounces, or 200 g; see Notes)

1 medium lemon, for zesting and juicing, divided

3 tablespoons olive oil

1 pinch fleur de sel or sea salt flakes

Black pepper

SALADE DE LENTILLES
AVEC CAROTTES RÔTIES ET SAUCE AU YAOURT À L'AIL

Here's a versatile salad recipe, perfect for all seasons, featuring vibrant spice-infused roasted carrots and French green lentils.

YIELD 2 SERVINGS
PREP TIME 15 MINUTES
COOK TIME 40 MINUTES

LENTILS

½ cup (100 g) dried French green lentils (see Note on page 68)

2 tablespoons olive oil

¼ cup (13 g) finely chopped fresh flat-leaf parsley

¼ cup (13 g) finely chopped fresh mint

1 small lemon, for zesting and juicing

Fleur de sel or sea salt flakes

Black pepper

ROASTED CARROTS

2 medium carrots, diagonally sliced

2 tablespoons olive oil

¼ teaspoon ground cumin

¼ teaspoon ground coriander

¼ teaspoon paprika

¼ teaspoon garlic powder

Salt and black pepper

GARLIC-YOGURT SAUCE

⅔ cup (160 g) plain Greek yogurt

1 clove garlic, minced

1 tablespoon olive oil

1 tablespoon fresh lemon juice

Fleur de sel or sea salt flakes

FOR GARNISHING

Black pepper

Fresh mint leaves, for garnishing

Fresh flat-leaf parsley leaves, for garnishing

1   **TO MAKE THE LENTILS:** Fill a large pot with cold water and add the lentils. Bring to a boil over high heat, then reduce the heat to medium and let simmer for 30 to 35 minutes, until the lentils are tender. Drain the lentils and rinse under cold water to stop the cooking process.

2   **MEANWHILE, MAKE THE ROASTED CARROTS:** Preheat the oven to 390°F (200°C) on the convection setting. Line a baking sheet with parchment paper.

continued on page 68

3 Add all the carrot ingredients to a medium bowl and toss until the carrots are evenly coated. Spread out the carrots in a single layer on the prepared baking sheet. Roast for 20 to 25 minutes, until tender and lightly browned. Let the carrots cool slightly so that they are no longer steaming.

4 Add the cooked lentils, 2 tablespoons oil, parsley, mint, grated lemon zest (reserving a little for garnishing), and juice from half of the lemon to the same bowl the carrots were mixed in. Season with salt and pepper and mix until well combined.

5 **TO MAKE THE GARLIC-YOGURT SAUCE:** In a small bowl, mix all the sauce ingredients until well combined.

6 Arrange the seasoned lentils on a serving plate, top with the roasted carrots and garlic-yogurt sauce, and garnish with the reserved lemon zest, pepper, and mint and parsley leaves. Serve immediately.

———

note To save time, replace the dried green lentils with 1 cup (250 g) of green or brown canned lentils.

SALADE DE PATATES DOUCES ET ROQUETTE

À LA VINAIGRETTE AU CITRON ET AU TAHINI

In modern French cuisine, we like to mix classic elements with nontraditional flavors, such as tahini and feta, in this case. This salad perfectly illustrates this balance, pairing the sweetness of roasted sweet potatoes with the peppery arugula, creamy feta, and crunchy pecans, all topped with a tangy tahini dressing.

YIELD 4 SERVINGS
PREP TIME 10 MINUTES
COOK TIME 40 MINUTES

PICKLED RED ONIONS (SEE NOTE ON PAGE 71)

½ cup (120 ml) apple cider vinegar

¼ cup (55 g) brown sugar

1 teaspoon salt

3 small red onions, thinly sliced

SALAD

1 large sweet potato, peeled and cut into ½-inch (about 1.5 cm) cubes

1 can (15 ounces, or 425 g) chickpeas, drained

½ teaspoon paprika

½ teaspoon ground cumin

½ teaspoon garlic powder

¼ teaspoon chile powder

Salt and black pepper

2 tablespoons olive oil

4 cups (140 g) mixed salad greens

4 cups (80 g) arugula

⅓ cup (35 g) pecan halves

7 ounces (200 g) feta cheese, crumbled

LEMON-TAHINI DRESSING

3 tablespoons tahini

3 tablespoons cold water

2 tablespoons fresh lemon juice

2 tablespoons olive oil

½ clove garlic, minced

1 teaspoon agave syrup or honey

¼ teaspoon salt

Black pepper

continued on page 71

1 **TO MAKE THE PICKLED RED ONIONS:** In a small saucepan, combine the vinegar, brown sugar, and 1 teaspoon salt with 1 cup (240 ml) of water. Heat over medium until the sugar dissolves. Place the sliced red onions in a jar and pour the liquid over them. Let cool to room temperature, then seal the jar and refrigerate for up to 2 weeks. (They can be used after 30 minutes but are best after 2 hours.)

2 **TO MAKE THE SALAD:** Preheat the oven to 390°F (200°C) on the convection setting. Line a baking sheet with parchment paper.

3 In a large bowl, combine the sweet potato, chickpeas, paprika, cumin, garlic powder, chili powder, salt and pepper to taste, and oil. Mix well to coat evenly. Spread the potatoes and chickpeas on the prepared baking sheet in a single layer. Bake for 25 to 30 minutes, until the potatoes are fork-tender.

4 **MEANWHILE, MAKE THE LEMON-TAHINI DRESSING:** In a small bowl, whisk together all the dressing ingredients until well combined, adjusting the consistency with water as needed.

5 Arrange the salad greens and arugula on a serving plate. Top with the roasted sweet potatoes and chickpeas and sprinkle with the pecans, feta, and pickled red onions to taste. Add half of the dressing, or to taste, and toss well. Serve immediately with the remaining dressing on the side.

———

note If you don't have time to make the pickled red onions, you can thinly slice half of a small red onion for topping.

SALADE DE POULET GRILLÉ
AUX GRAINES DE SARRASIN ET AU PESTO

This salad with grilled chicken, buckwheat groats, and pesto is both healthy and satiating. Buckwheat is a grain that is not commonly used, yet it's very quick to cook, naturally gluten-free, and travels well for meals on the go.

YIELD 2 SERVINGS
PREP TIME 10 MINUTES
COOK TIME 15 MINUTES

½ cup (100 g) buckwheat groats, rinsed (or substitute with pearl couscous, bulgur, or orzo pasta)

1 teaspoon coarse salt

2 boneless, skinless chicken breasts

Salt and black pepper

½ teaspoon smoked paprika

½ teaspoon garlic powder

1 teaspoon dried oregano

2 tablespoons olive oil, plus more for cooking and drizzling

¼ cup (35 g) pine nuts

1 cup (145 g) halved cherry tomatoes

1 cup (130 g) ¼-inch-diced (6 cm) cucumber

2 cups (40 g) arugula

⅓ cup (80 g) basil pesto or Pistou Sauce (page 48)

1 In a small saucepan, combine the buckwheat groats and coarse salt with 1 cup (240 ml) of water. Bring to a boil, then reduce the heat to medium-low and cook for 10 to 15 minutes, until the groats are tender. Drain, rinse under cold water, and drain again.

2 While the groats cook, season the chicken breasts with salt and pepper. In a small bowl, mix the paprika, garlic powder, oregano, and 2 tablespoons oil until well combined. Brush the chicken breasts with this marinade on both sides.

3 In a medium dry skillet (without any oil), toast the pine nuts over medium heat for about 5 minutes, or until golden brown, stirring continuously to avoid burning. Remove them from the pan.

4 In the same skillet, heat a drizzle of oil over medium-high heat. Sear the chicken breasts for 4 to 5 minutes per side, until well browned. Reduce the heat to medium-low and continue cooking until the internal temperature of the chicken reaches 165°F (74°C). Transfer the chicken breasts to a cutting board and slice against the grain using a sharp knife.

5 In a large salad bowl, combine the cooked buckwheat, cherry tomatoes, cucumber, and arugula. Add the pesto and mix well. Divide the salad between two plates, top with slices of grilled chicken, and finish with some toasted pine nuts and a drizzle of oil. Serve immediately.

Niçoise-Style Salad with Tuna Tataki

SALADE FAÇON NIÇOISE AU TATAKI DE THON

Here's a slightly more sophisticated version of the famous salade niçoise. Instead of canned tuna, I have opted for tuna tataki, a Japanese cooking method that involves lightly searing the tuna so that it remains raw inside.

1 **TO MAKE THE SALAD:** Bring a large pot of salted water to a boil. Prepare a bowl of cold water with ice cubes for an ice bath. Cook the green beans in the boiling water for 5 to 10 minutes, until crisp-tender. Using a slotted spoon, transfer the beans to the ice bath for 2 minutes, then drain. In the same water the beans were cooked in, cook the potatoes over medium heat for 20 minutes, or until fork-tender. Remove from the pot with a slotted spoon. Finally, cook the eggs in the same water over medium heat for 10 to 12 minutes, until hard-boiled. Rinse the eggs under cold water, peel, and slice into quarters.

2 Season the tuna steaks with salt and pepper. Place the sesame seeds on a plate and coat the steaks all over with them. Heat the 1 tablespoon oil in a large skillet over medium-high heat. Add the tuna steaks and sear for 1 minute per side; the steaks will be raw inside. Transfer to a cutting board and, using a sharp knife, cut the steaks into strips no more than ½ inch (1.5 cm) thick.

3 **TO MAKE THE LEMON-GARLIC VINAIGRETTE:** In a small bowl, whisk together the lemon juice, mustard, and salt to taste until the salt dissolves. Add the garlic and gradually pour in the ¼ cup (60 ml) oil while whisking until well combined. Season with black pepper.

4 In a large salad bowl, combine the salad greens, cherry tomatoes, potatoes, eggs, and green beans. Add all the vinaigrette and toss well. Divide the salad between two plates and top with slices of tuna. Serve immediately.

YIELD 4 SERVINGS
PREP TIME 10 MINUTES
COOK TIME 40 MINUTES

SALAD

Salt

7 ounces (200 g) fresh green beans, stems trimmed

16 baby potatoes

2 medium eggs

2 or 3 large tuna steaks (21 ounces, or 600 g; make sure they are fresh and safe to consume raw; if you have any doubts, consult the fishmonger)

Black pepper

¼ cup (35 g) mixed white and black sesame seeds

1 tablespoon olive oil

7 ounces (200 g) mixed salad greens

14 cherry tomatoes, cut in half

LEMON-GARLIC VINAIGRETTE

2 tablespoons fresh lemon juice

1 teaspoon Dijon mustard

Salt

½ clove garlic, minced

¼ cup (60 ml) olive oil

Black pepper

SALADE DE POMMES DE TERRE RÔTIES
AU CONCOMBRE ET VINAIGRETTE AU YAOURT

What I love about this salad is the combination of crispy, oven-roasted potatoes with the freshness of cucumber and dill, all tossed in a light, creamy yogurt sauce.

YIELD 2 OR 3 SERVINGS
PREP TIME 10 MINUTES
COOK TIME 45 MINUTES

SALAD

21 ounces (600 g) baby potatoes, cut into quarters

3 tablespoons olive oil

½ teaspoon plus 1 pinch salt, divided

½ teaspoon black pepper

½ teaspoon smoked paprika

½ teaspoon garlic powder

½ English cucumber, cut in half lengthwise, then thinly sliced into half-moons

2 green onions, thinly sliced

1 cup (50 g) chopped fresh dill

1 cup (50 g) chopped fresh flat-leaf parsley

YOGURT DRESSING

½ cup (120 g) plain yogurt (3.5% fat)

1 tablespoon olive oil

1 tablespoon fresh lemon juice

1 tablespoon Dijon mustard

1 pinch salt

1 **TO MAKE THE SALAD:** Preheat the oven to 390°F (200°C) on the convection setting. Line a baking sheet with parchment paper.

2 In a large bowl, combine the potatoes, 3 tablespoons oil, ½ teaspoon each salt and pepper, paprika, and garlic powder and toss well to coat the potatoes evenly. Spread the potatoes on the prepared baking sheet in a single layer. Roast for 45 to 50 minutes, until the potatoes are golden and crispy.

3 **MEANWHILE, MAKE THE YOGURT DRESSING:** In a small bowl, whisk together all the dressing ingredients until well combined.

4 In a large bowl, combine the cucumber, onions, dill, parsley, and remaining pinch of salt and mix well. Add the roasted potatoes, then toss gently with all the yogurt dressing. Serve immediately so that the warm potatoes remain crisp.

MEAT MAINS

One-Pan Stuffed Tomatoes Provençale-Style with Rice

TOMATES FARCIES
À LA PROVENÇALE ET RIZ

This is a great classic from Provence. What makes it particularly popular is its simplicity of preparation—everything comes together effortlessly in a single dish.

YIELD 4 SERVINGS
PREP TIME 20 MINUTES
COOK TIME 45 MINUTES

2 slices white bread
(such as sandwich bread)

¼ cup (60 ml) milk

4 large tomatoes or 6 medium tomatoes (I like to use Oxheart tomatoes)

Salt and black pepper

1 pound (455 g) mix
ground beef and pork

1 medium egg

½ cup (18 g) finely chopped curly parsley, plus ¼ cup (9 g) for garnishing

2 large cloves garlic, minced

1 small white onion,
finely chopped

2 tablespoons Herbes de Provence (page 11)

1 pinch Espelette pepper
(or use less cayenne pepper)

1¼ cups (250 g)
long-grain white rice

2 tablespoons olive oil

1 Preheat the oven to 350°F (180°C) on the convection setting.

2 Place the bread slices in a small bowl, add the milk, and let soak for 5 minutes.

3 Cut off the tops of the tomatoes by about ½ inch (1.5 cm), reserving them. Using a spoon, carefully remove the flesh of the tomatoes, transferring it to a bowl to use later. Season the insides of the tomatoes with salt and black pepper.

4 In a large bowl, combine the ground meat, soaked bread slices, egg, parsley, garlic, and onion. Season generously with salt and black pepper and add the herbes de Provence and Espelette pepper. Mix by hand until the mixture is homogeneous.

5 Spread the rice in a large baking dish and add 2¼ cups (540 ml) of water. Season with salt and black pepper. Add the reserved tomato flesh, finely chopping it first if necessary, and mix well.

6 Fill the tomatoes with the meat stuffing, then carefully place the reserved tops on each one. Arrange the stuffed tomatoes on the bed of rice in the baking dish. Drizzle with the olive oil.

7 Bake for 40 to 45 minutes, until the tomatoes are tender and the stuffing is cooked through. Garnish with the chopped parsley and serve immediately.

note This dish can easily be made vegetarian by replacing the ground meat with a plant-based meat or a mixture of cooked lentils and mushrooms.

Milk-Roasted Pork with Sage

RÔTI DE PORC AU LAIT
ET À LA SAUGE

This pork-roast recipe is perfect to make for a Sunday meal. Roasting the pork in milk makes it super tender, and the sage adds a lovely lemony, herbaceous flavor. Pair with mashed potatoes or rice.

1   Remove the pork roast from the refrigerator at least 1 hour before cooking. When ready to cook, season the roast on all sides with salt.

2   In a large Dutch oven, heat the oil over medium-high heat. Add the roast and sear on each side for about 2 minutes, or until evenly caramelized. Remove the pork from the pan. To the same Dutch oven, add the onion, garlic cloves, and butter over medium heat. Let the butter melt and stir well with a wooden spoon to loosen the browned bits from the seared pork from the bottom of the pan.

3   Return the roast to the pot, pour in the milk, and add the bay leaves, thyme, sage, and nutmeg. Cover with the lid and let simmer over low heat for 1 hour and 30 minutes to 2 hours, until the internal temperature reaches 135°F (57°C; for medium) or 158°F (70°C; for well done). Turn the roast every 30 minutes to make sure it cooks evenly. Remove the pork from the Dutch oven, transfer it to a cutting board, and cover it with parchment paper or aluminum foil. Let it rest for 10 minutes.

4   Meanwhile, strain the milk sauce through a sieve. Return the liquid to the Dutch oven and cook over medium-high heat for 15 minutes, or until the sauce reduces and thickens. If you prefer a thicker sauce, dissolve the cornstarch with the cold water, then pour the slurry into the sauce. Bring to a boil and stir continuously until sauce has the desired consistency. Season the sauce with salt and pepper.

5   If the roast is tied, remove the string. Slice the roast, then return the slices to the sauce for a minute to reheat. Serve with the milk sauce.

YIELD 8 SERVINGS
PREP TIME 10 MINUTES, PLUS
1 HOUR 10 MINUTES RESTING
COOK TIME 2 HOURS

3⅓ pounds (1.5 kg) pork roast (shoulder), tied or untied

Salt

2 tablespoons olive oil

1 medium white onion, thinly sliced

10 cloves garlic, skins on

2 tablespoons unsalted butter

4¼ cups (1 L) cold whole milk

2 bay leaves

6 sprigs fresh thyme

10 leaves fresh sage

1 pinch ground nutmeg

2 tablespoons cornstarch (optional)

¼ cup (60 ml) cold water (optional)

Black pepper

POULET DU DIMANCHE
AU CITRON ET LÉGUMES RÔTIS

In France, the traditional Sunday meal is roast chicken and potatoes. To freshen up this classic dish, I like to coat my chicken with an easy lemon butter and add a few vegetables, especially fennel.

YIELD 4 SERVINGS
PREP TIME 15 MINUTES
COOK TIME 1 HOUR
20 MINUTES

LEMON BUTTER

¼ cup (60 g) unsalted butter, at room temperature

1 medium lemon, for zesting and juicing

1 pinch salt

ROAST CHICKEN

1 whole chicken (4 pounds, or 1.8 kg), trussed or untrussed

Salt and black pepper

1 medium yellow onion, cut into quarters

6 cloves garlic, skins on, divided

2 sprigs fresh rosemary

7 sprigs fresh thyme, divided, plus more for garnishing

14 ounces (400 g) baby potatoes

3 small carrots, cut into large pieces

1 large fennel bulb, hard end and fronds removed and cut into 6 wedges

2 medium red onions, cut into quarters

2 tablespoons olive oil

1 **TO MAKE THE LEMON BUTTER:** Place the butter in a small bowl. Add the grated lemon zest, 1 tablespoon lemon juice, and pinch of salt and mix well with a fork to lightly whip the butter. Squeeze the remaining juice from the lemon into a separate bowl to use later. Cut the squeezed lemon into 4 slices.

2 **TO MAKE THE ROAST CHICKEN:** Preheat the oven to 390°F (200°C) on the convection setting. Season the inside of the chicken with salt and pepper. Fill the cavity with the yellow onion, 3 garlic cloves, 2 reserved lemon slices, rosemary sprigs, and 3 thyme sprigs. Brush the skin of the chicken with the lemon butter, massaging it all over.

3 Add the potatoes, carrots, fennel, and red onions to a large bowl along with the oil, reserved lemon juice, and salt and pepper to taste and toss well. Transfer the vegetables to a large oven-safe baking dish and arrange the remaining 2 lemon slices, 3 garlic cloves, and 4 thyme sprigs around the vegetables.

4 Place the chicken on top of the vegetables, breast side up. Roast for 1 hour and 20 minutes, or until the internal temperature reaches 165°F (74°C), turning the chicken after 30 minutes, and then again after another 30 minutes, basting it as often as possible with the cooking juices. Remove from the oven and let rest for 10 minutes, covering it with aluminum foil or parchment paper. Remove the chicken and vegetables from the baking dish and pour the cooking juices into a small bowl. Remove the string from the chicken, if trussed, and cut it into pieces. Serve the chicken with some of the vegetables and the cooking juices. Garnish with a little fresh thyme.

FILET MIGNON DE PORC
AU BACON ET AUX HERBES

Here's an easy-to-prepare pork tenderloin recipe that's sure to impress your guests. The herbs add a tasty and delicately refreshing Mediterranean touch.

1   Preheat the oven to 390°F (200°C) on the convection setting.

2   Remove the rosemary and thyme leaves from the stems, then finely chop them along with the sage leaves.

3   Season the pork tenderloin with salt and pepper. Evenly sprinkle the chopped herbs over the tenderloin, reserving some for garnishing. Wrap the tenderloin with the bacon strips, slightly overlapping them as you place them crosswise around the tenderloin. Secure the ends by tucking them underneath the tenderloin.

4   Drizzle the oil in a baking dish large enough to hold the tenderloin. Place the tenderloin in the dish, pour in the white wine, and add the garlic cloves. Bake for 35 to 40 minutes, until the internal temperature of the pork reaches 160°F (71°C). Cover with aluminum foil or parchment paper if the bacon starts to blacken while baking. Let rest for 5 minutes.

5   Slice the tenderloin, sprinkle with the reserved herbs, and serve with the sauce collected from the baking dish (see Note).

———

note   Complete the meal by serving this tenderloin with the Rustic Gratin Dauphinois (page 164), the Green Beans with Crunchy Honey Almonds (page 163), or the Olive Oil and Lemon Mashed Potatoes (page 156).

YIELD 4 SERVINGS
PREP TIME 15 MINUTES
COOK TIME 45 MINUTES

3 sprigs fresh rosemary

10 sprigs fresh thyme

8 leaves fresh sage

1¼ pounds (550 g) pork tenderloin

Salt and black pepper

10 slices bacon

1 tablespoon olive oil

¼ cup (60 ml) dry white wine

3 large cloves garlic, skins on

Beef Stew with Heirloom Vegetables

POT-AU-FEU
AUX LÉGUMES ANCIENS

This is one of the ultimate French comfort foods! Pot-au-feu is a warming, homemade beef broth served with winter vegetables. To spice up this recipe, I like to add heirloom vegetables, such as yellow carrots, orange beets, and parsley root.

YIELD 5 OR 6 SERVINGS
PREP TIME 15 MINUTES
COOK TIME 5 HOURS

BEEF STEW

1 large onion,
peeled and cut in half

2 dark green leek leaves

2 bay leaves

5 sprigs fresh thyme

1¾ pounds (800 g) beef (tail,
chuck, or cheek, or a mix of
these cuts), cut into 3-inch
(7.5 cm) pieces

1½ pounds (700 g)
beef short ribs

Cold water
(about 14 cups, or 3.5 L)

1 large carrot, peeled, cut in half
crosswise, and tied together
with a kitchen string

2 teaspoons mixed white
and black peppercorns

2 cloves garlic, skins on

Salt (see Notes on page 90)

**HEIRLOOM VEGETABLES
(SEE NOTES ON PAGE 90)**

6 medium starchy potatoes,
peeled and cut in half

½ small head green cabbage,
cut into quarters

2 large leeks, white parts only,
cut in half, then sliced into long
pieces

2 medium orange beets,
peeled and cut into 8 wedges

2 large yellow carrots, peeled
and sliced into thick rounds

1 large parsley root, peeled,
cut in half crosswise, and then
cut into quarters lengthwise

FOR SERVING

Whole grain Dijon mustard

1   **TO MAKE THE BEEF STEW:** In a dry skillet (without any oil) over high heat, char the onion halves on their cut sides until lightly blackened. (The onion will not be eaten; it is used to give a more intense flavor to the soup.)

2   Tie the leek leaves, bay leaves, and thyme sprigs together with a kitchen string for a bouquet garni.

——————

continued on page 90

3   Place the beef pieces and short ribs in a large pot and cover with cold water. Bring to a boil and skim off any foam that has formed on the surface to remove excess fat. Add the bouquet garni, charred onion halves, tied carrot, peppercorns, and garlic cloves to the pot. Cover with the lid and cook for 4 to 5 hours over medium-low heat, until the meat becomes fork-tender. Continue to skim off any foam about every hour if necessary. Remove the meat from the pot.

4   Set a fine-mesh strainer over a large bowl, then carefully filter the broth through it to remove any impurities, the bouquet garni, onion halves, and peppercorns. Return the filtered broth and meat to the pot. Season the broth with salt. (At this stage, you can turn off the heat until you are ready to cook the vegetables in the next step and serve. You can even make this the day before and cook the vegetables before serving.)

5   **TO MAKE THE HEIRLOOM VEGETABLES:** About 1 hour before serving, add all the heirloom vegetables to the broth and cook over medium-low heat until the vegetables are tender. This should take 45 minutes to up to 1 hour.

6   Serve 1 or 2 pieces of meat with a variety of vegetables in shallow bowls and pour the broth over them. Serve with some Dijon mustard on the side (I like to add a small teaspoon of mustard to a piece of meat and eat it that way).

notes

It is recommended that you leave the meat and water unsalted, to allow the flavors to develop. Only add salt to the broth at the end of cooking in step 4.

Other vegetables to use in this stew include yellow turnips, purple turnips, parsnips, black radishes, and celery root.

You can prepare the broth and meat the day before and leave them to infuse, covered, in the fridge. The flavor will develop even more.

NAVARRIN D'AGNEAU PRINTANIER

Another classic of French cuisine, this stew is traditionally served in spring and especially on Easter. I especially like the crunchy spring vegetables that are added at the end of cooking, bringing a freshness to this lamb stew.

YIELD 6 TO 8 SERVINGS
PREP TIME 20 MINUTES
COOK TIME 1 HOUR AND 15 MINUTES

LAMB STEW

3 sprigs fresh rosemary

4 sprigs fresh thyme

2⅔ pounds (1.2 kg) lamb (leg, shoulder, or neck), excess fat trimmed and cut into 1½-inch (4 cm) cubes

Salt and black pepper

2 tablespoons olive oil

2 tablespoons unsalted butter

1 large yellow onion, thinly sliced

2 cloves garlic, skins on

2 medium carrots, peeled and sliced into thin rounds

3 tablespoons tomato paste

2 tablespoons all-purpose flour

½ cup (120 ml) dry white wine

2 cups (480 ml) beef or chicken broth

1 cup (240 ml) water

SPRING VEGETABLES

1 pound (455 g) baby potatoes

2 cups fresh (290 g) or frozen (270 g) peas

2 cups fresh (230 g) or frozen (220 g) green beans, stems trimmed if fresh

GLAZED PEARL ONIONS

18 pearl onions, peeled

1 teaspoon granulated sugar

¼ teaspoon salt

½ cup (120 ml) cold water

2 tablespoons unsalted butter, cut into small pieces

1 **TO MAKE THE LAMB STEW:** Tie the rosemary and thyme sprigs together with kitchen string for a bouquet garni.

2 Pat the lamb cubes dry with paper towels, then season generously with salt and pepper on all sides.

3 In a large Dutch oven, heat the oil over medium-high heat. Add the lamb and sear until well caramelized on all sides. If necessary, do this step in two or three batches to avoid overcrowding the pot and to ensure a nice caramelization. Remove the meat from the pot. Also remove any excess oil and fat from the pot.

———

continued on page 93

4   Add the butter, yellow onion, garlic cloves, and carrots to the Dutch oven and sauté over medium-high heat for 2 minutes, or until the onion begins to brown. Return the lamb to the pot, then add the tomato paste and mix well. Add the flour and cook for 2 minutes, stirring well.

5   Pour in the white wine and deglaze by scraping the bottom of the pot with a wooden spoon to release any browned bits. Add the broth, 1 cup (240 ml) of water, and the bouquet garni and bring to a boil. Once the liquid starts boiling, immediately reduce the heat to the lowest setting. Let simmer for 1 hour to 1 hour and 30 minutes, stirring occasionally, until the meat is fork-tender. Do not cover to allow the sauce to reduce.

6   **MEANWHILE, MAKE THE SPRING VEGETABLES (SEE NOTES):** Salt a large pot of cold water, then add the potatoes and bring to a boil. Once boiling, reduce the heat to medium and cook the potatoes for 20 minutes, or until fork-tender. Remove with a slotted spoon. In the same pot, cook the peas over medium heat for 5 minutes if fresh or 2 minutes if frozen, or until crisp-tender. Remove with a slotted spoon and optionally place them in an ice bath to retain their green color. Finally, in the same pot, cook the green beans over medium heat for 10 minutes if fresh or 5 minutes if frozen, or until crisp-tender. Remove with a slotted spoon and optionally place them in an ice bath to retain their green color.

7   **MEANWHILE, MAKE THE GLAZED PEARL ONIONS:** Place the pearl onions side by side in a large skillet or pot (they should not overlap), then sprinkle with the sugar and ¼ teaspoon salt. Add the cold water, then distribute the butter pieces over the onions. Cut a circle of parchment paper the diameter of the pan and cover the onions with it; this will allow the water to evaporate and steam the onions to cook them slowly. Place the pan on the stovetop over medium-low heat and cook the onions for 10 to 15 minutes, until the water evaporates and the onions are tender.

8   Right before serving, transfer the cooked potatoes, peas, green beans, and glazed onions to the Dutch oven. Serve the stew in shallow bowls (see Notes).

notes   To save time, you can cook the spring vegetables directly in the stew. Add the potatoes about 30 minutes before the end of the stew's cooking time, depending on their size, and add the peas and green beans 5 to 10 minutes before the end of cooking. Cooking the vegetables separately keeps them crunchy and adds freshness to the stew.

You can enjoy this stew on its own or served over mashed potatoes.

This dish tastes even better the next day. So, feel free to prepare it a day in advance and reheat it on the stovetop over medium-low heat when ready to serve.

Marinated Pork Chops with Herbes de Provence

CÔTES DE PORC MARINÉES
AUX HERBES DE PROVENCE

Often served at summer barbecues in France, these pork chops are marinated with herbes de Provence, olive oil, and garlic, a classic combination. For this recipe, I pan-sear the pork chops, but you can also grill them. The addition of tomato polenta with Parmesan complements these pork chops well.

YIELD 4 SERVINGS
PREP TIME 5 MINUTES,
PLUS 2 HOURS MARINATING
COOK TIME 20 MINUTES

MARINATED PORK CHOPS

4 bone-in pork chops

Salt and black pepper

¼ cup (60 ml) olive oil,
plus more for cooking

1 tablespoon fresh lemon juice

2 tablespoons
Herbes de Provence (page 11)

4 cloves garlic,
skins on and smashed

4 small branches
cherry tomatoes

TOMATO POLENTA

1 can (14 ounces, or 411 g) whole
peeled or crushed tomatoes

1 tablespoon olive oil

1 cup (160 g) fine polenta

Salt and black pepper

⅔ cup (80 g) grated
Parmesan cheese

2 tablespoons unsalted butter

1 **TO MAKE THE MARINATED PORK CHOPS:** Season the pork chops with salt and pepper on both sides. Place them in an airtight container and add the ¼ cup (60 ml) oil, lemon juice, herbes de Provence, and garlic cloves. Seal, shake, and let marinate in the refrigerator for at least 2 hours, or overnight.

2 **TO MAKE THE TOMATO POLENTA:** Place the tomatoes in a blender with 2 cups (480 ml) of water and blend until the consistency of tomato juice. In a medium saucepan, heat the 1 tablespoon oil over medium heat. Add the polenta and sauté for 1 minute. Add the tomato-water mixture, season with salt and pepper, and cook for about 15 minutes, stirring constantly, or until the polenta separates from the pan's edges. Stir in the Parmesan and butter right before serving.

3 Meanwhile, heat a cast-iron grill pan or large skillet over medium-high heat. Add a drizzle of oil and the pork chops, working in batches if necessary to avoid overcrowding the pan. Sear on one side for 3 to 4 minutes without moving them, then flip and sear for another 3 minutes, or until the internal temperature reaches 150°F (65°C) for medium rare or 160°F (70°C) for well done. Remove the pork chops from the pan and let rest for 5 minutes under parchment paper or aluminum foil. Sear the cherry tomatoes on their branches in the same pan for 3 minutes, or until wilted. Serve the pork chops with the polenta and grilled tomatoes.

Braised Beef with Red Wine and Carrots

BOEUF BRAISÉ
AU VIN ROUGE ET CAROTTES

This braised beef is a delicious alternative to boeuf bourguignon, as it's rich in flavor and requires little preparation. It tastes even better when prepared a day in advance and reheated.

1 Preheat the oven to 320°F (160 °C) on the convection setting. Pat the beef cubes dry with paper towels, then season with salt and pepper on all sides.

2 In a large Dutch oven or braiser pan, heat the oil over medium-high heat. Add the beef and sear until well caramelized on all sides, cooking in batches if necessary to avoid overcrowding the pot. Remove the beef from the pot. Add the onions, shallot, carrots, and celery to the same pot and sauté over medium-high heat for 2 minutes, or until the onion starts to brown. Add the garlic and tomato paste and mix well. Stir in the flour and cook for 1 minute. Pour in the red wine and broth and deglaze by scraping the bottom of the pot with a wooden spoon to release any browned bits. Return the beef to the pot and season with a generous pinch each of salt and pepper.

3 Tie the bay leaves and thyme and rosemary sprigs together with a kitchen string for a bouquet garni. Place it in the pot. Cover the pot with the lid and carefully transfer to the oven. Cook for 3 to 4 hours, until the beef is fork-tender, stirring occasionally, every 1 hour and 30 minutes, for even cooking. If the meat seems too tough, let it cook for 1 more hour; the longer the beef cooks, the more tender it will be. If you prefer a thicker sauce, dissolve the cornstarch with the cold water, then pour the slurry into the pot and heat over medium heat on the stovetop, stirring continuously until the sauce thickens.

4 Serve the stew in shallow bowls with polenta, mashed potatoes, or pasta, as the dish is quite rich on its own.

YIELD 6 TO 8 SERVINGS
PREP TIME 30 MINUTES
COOK TIME 4 HOURS

3 pounds (1.3 kg) beef chuck or blade roast, cut into 2-inch (5 cm) cubes

Salt and black pepper

2 tablespoons olive oil

2 medium yellow onions, thinly sliced

1 medium shallot, finely chopped

4 medium carrots, sliced into thick rounds

1 celery rib, cut into ¼-inch (6 mm) dice

3 cloves garlic, minced

2 tablespoons tomato paste

2 tablespoons all-purpose flour

1 bottle (750 ml) red wine

2 cups (480 ml) beef broth

2 bay leaves

4 sprigs fresh thyme

1 sprig fresh rosemary

2 tablespoons cornstarch (optional)

¼ cup (60 ml) cold water (optional)

Polenta, mashed potatoes, or pasta, for serving

Creamy Tarragon and Mushroom Chicken

SUPRÊMES DE POULET
À L'ESTRAGON ET CHAMPIGNONS

Tarragon is an herb that is sometimes overlooked, but in this recipe, it gives the entire dish its complexity. This is a simple recipe that must not be missed! Enjoy the chicken and sauce over white rice or pasta.

YIELD 4 SERVINGS
PREP TIME 10 MINUTES
COOK TIME 30 MINUTES

CHICKEN

4 boneless, skin-on chicken breasts (about 6½ ounces, or 80 g, each)

Salt and black pepper

¼ cup (30 g) all-purpose flour

2 tablespoons olive oil

CREAMY SAUCE

2½ cups (250 g) sliced button mushrooms

Olive oil (optional)

Salt

1 large shallot, minced

2 tablespoons unsalted butter

¼ cup (30 g) all-purpose flour

¼ cup (60 ml) dry white wine

2 cups (480 ml) chicken broth

⅔ cup (160 ml) heavy whipping cream

2 cups (60 g) baby spinach or chopped spinach leaves

⅓ cup (17 g) chopped fresh tarragon

1 **TO MAKE THE CHICKEN:** Season the chicken breasts with salt and pepper on both sides. Place the flour in a shallow bowl and dredge the breasts in the flour to coat, shaking off any excess flour.

2 In a large skillet or Dutch oven, heat the oil over medium-high heat. Add the chicken breasts and sear for 3 minutes per side, or until golden brown, without moving them while they cook. Remove the chicken breasts from the pan.

3 **TO MAKE THE CREAMY SAUCE:** Add the mushrooms to the same skillet the chicken was cooked in, adding a bit more oil if necessary, and sauté over medium-high heat for 5 to 10 minutes, until they are tender and browned. Season with salt and remove from the pan.

4 To the same skillet, add the shallot and sauté over medium heat for 2 minutes. Add the butter and let it melt, then add the flour and whisk to create a light-colored paste (roux). Pour in the white wine and deglaze by scraping the bottom of the pan with a wooden spoon to release any browned bits. Add the broth, 1 cup (240 ml) at a time, stirring continuously to create a creamy sauce. Return the chicken breasts to the pan and let cook over medium heat for 15 to 20 minutes, until the internal temperature reaches at least 165°F (74°C), turning them occasionally for even cooking. Just before serving, add the cream, sautéed mushrooms, spinach, and tarragon. Stir well and cook for 2 minutes, or until the cream is warm and the spinach is wilted. Taste and adjust the salt and pepper if necessary.

5 Serve the chicken breasts immediately with the creamy sauce.

Steak with Garlic, Lemon, and Herb Butter

STEAK AU BEURRE D'AIL, CITRON ET HERBES

This recipe is a summer favorite, perfect for outdoor dining. The citrusy herb butter adds a burst of flavor to the juicy steak, while the grilled romaine brings a refreshing twist. It's a quick and easy meal that feels special, making it ideal for both a weeknight dinner or a relaxed gathering with friends.

1 **TO MAKE THE GARLIC, LEMON, AND HERB BUTTER:** In a medium bowl, mix the butter, grated lemon zest, 1 tablespoon lemon juice, garlic, thyme, lemon thyme, rosemary, and ½ teaspoon fleur de sel with a fork until well combined.

2 **TO MAKE THE STEAKS:** Season the steaks generously with salt and pepper on both sides. Heat a large skillet or cast-iron grill pan over medium-high heat, then add the oil. When the oil is sizzling, add the steaks and cook for 3 to 4 minutes per side for medium rare, or to your desired doneness. During the last minute of cooking, add 2 tablespoons of the garlic, lemon, and herb butter to the skillet, basting the steaks with the melted butter. Remove the steaks from the skillet and let them rest for a few minutes before serving.

3 **TO MAKE THE GRILLED ROMAINE:** Brush the cut sides of the romaine halves with the oil. Place the romaine halves, cut sides down, in the same skillet over medium-high heat. Grill for about 3 minutes per side, or until charred and slightly wilted. Remove and season with fleur de sel and pepper.

4 Right before serving, add a slice of the butter on top of each steak. Serve immediately with the grilled romaine.

note You can serve the leftover butter with a baguette or use it to sauté vegetables.

YIELD 2 SERVINGS
PREP TIME 15 MINUTES, PLUS 1 HOUR CHILLING
COOK TIME 12 MINUTES

GARLIC, LEMON, AND HERB BUTTER

⅔ cup (160 g) unsalted butter, at room temperature

1 lemon for zesting and juicing

1 clove garlic, minced

½ teaspoon finely chopped fresh thyme leaves

½ teaspoon finely chopped fresh lemon thyme leaves

½ teaspoon finely chopped fresh rosemary

½ teaspoon fleur de sel or sea salt flakes

STEAKS

2 steaks (such as sirloin or rib eye; about 7½ ounces, or 210 g, each)

Salt and black pepper

1 tablespoon olive oil

GRILLED ROMAINE

1 head romaine lettuce, cut in half lengthwise

1 tablespoon olive oil

Fleur de sel or sea salt flakes and black pepper

FISH
MAINS

TARTARE DE SAUMON
À L'ANETH ET AU POIVRE ROSE

You're probably familiar with beef tartare, but this salmon version is even better and a classic of French cuisine. I love combining salmon and dill, and I've added some pink peppercorns to give this tartare a slightly fruity, spicy note.

YIELD 4 SERVINGS
PREP TIME 15 MINUTES

1⅓ pounds (600 g) fresh skinless salmon fillets (see Notes)

1 tablespoon pink peppercorns, plus more for garnishing

1 medium lemon, for zesting and juicing, divided

2 tablespoons finely chopped red onion

2 tablespoons finely chopped fresh dill, plus more for garnishing

2 tablespoons roughly chopped capers

2 tablespoons olive oil, plus more for greasing

Fleur de sel or sea salt flakes

1 Pat the salmon fillets dry with paper towels. Cut the fillets into roughly ¼-inch (6 mm) cubes. (To make slicing easier, first place the salmon in the freezer for 10 minutes.)

2 Using a mortar and pestle, roughly crush the pink peppercorns to release their flavors.

3 In a medium bowl, combine the salmon, grated lemon zest, onion, dill, crushed peppercorns, and capers and mix well. Add the oil, 2 tablespoons lemon juice, and fleur de sel and mix well again.

4 Grease a 3-inch (7.5 cm) round cookie cutter with oil and place in the center of a plate. Fill it with one-quarter of the salmon tartare, pressing down to compact it. Carefully lift the mold. Repeat this step three more times with the remaining tartare.

5 Garnish with chopped dill and pink peppercorns. Serve immediately (see Notes).

———

notes

Make sure the salmon fillets are fresh and safe to consume raw; if you have any doubts, consult the fishmonger.

Serve this tartare with the Healthy Oven-Baked French Fries (page 160) and a green salad for a main course or with slices of toasted bread for a starter.

Cod Loins with Pistachio Crust

DOS DE CABILLAUD
EN CROÛTE DE PISTACHE

Here's a very simple way to cook cod fillets, combining the delicacy of this white fish with a delicious, crispy pistachio crust with Parmesan. For this recipe, I like to use cod loin, which is the thick, boneless central part of the fish. It is particularly flaky and tender.

1 Preheat the oven to 390°F (200°C) on the convection setting. Line a baking sheet with parchment paper or grease a baking dish with a little oil.

2 Pat the cod loin fillets dry with paper towels and season on both sides with salt. Place the fish fillets in the prepared pan.

3 In a small bowl, combine the pistachios, bread crumbs, Parmesan, and garlic. Season with salt and pepper, then add the ⅓ cup (80 ml) oil and mix well.

4 Spoon the pistachio mixture over the fish. (It doesn't matter if it falls off.)

5 Bake for 12 to 15 minutes, until the flesh is opaque and white and the crust is golden-brown.

6 Garnish the fillets with chopped dill and parsley and serve with lemon slices (see Notes). Use the crust that has fallen to the bottom of the pan as a topping for side dishes.

———

notes

This recipe can be made with any type of white fish, or even salmon fillets.

You can serve these cod loins with the Slow-Roasted Vegetable Ratatouille (page 168) and toasted bread or the Olive Oil and Lemon Mashed Potatoes (page 156).

YIELD 4 SERVINGS
PREP TIME 10 MINUTES
COOK TIME 12 MINUTES

⅓ cup (80 ml) olive oil, plus more for greasing (optional)

4 cod loin fillets (20 to 28 ounces, or 600 to 800 g; see Notes)

Salt

⅔ cup (75 g) unsalted pistachios, crushed

⅓ cup (50 g) bread crumbs

½ cup (60 g) grated Parmesan cheese

2 cloves garlic, minced

Black pepper

4 sprigs fresh dill, chopped, for garnishing

4 sprigs fresh flat-leaf parsley, chopped, for garnishing

1 small lemon, sliced, for serving

Tuna Meatballs in Tomato Sauce

BOULETTES DE THON
À LA SAUCE TOMATE

YIELD 4 SERVINGS
PREP TIME 15 MINUTES
COOK TIME 30 MINUTES

TUNA MEATBALLS

1½ slices white bread
(such as sandwich bread)

2 cans (7 ounces, or 200 g,
each) tuna, well drained

½ cup (60 g) grated
Parmesan cheese

2 medium eggs

1 clove garlic, minced

½ cup (18 g) finely chopped
fresh curly parsley

¼ teaspoon Espelette pepper
(or use less cayenne pepper)

Salt and black pepper

2 tablespoons olive oil

TOMATO SAUCE

1 tablespoon olive oil

1 small yellow onion,
finely chopped

3 cloves garlic, minced

½ teaspoon red pepper flakes

2 cans (14 ounces, or 400 g,
each) crushed tomatoes

2 bay leaves

1 teaspoon dried oregano

1 pinch salt

FOR GARNISHING
Finely chopped fresh
curly parsley

These meatballs made with canned tuna are a delicious alternative to traditional meatballs and ideal for a busy weeknight meal. Serve with the sauce over spaghetti or rice.

1   **TO MAKE THE TUNA MEATBALLS:** Preheat the oven to 390°F (200°C) on the convection setting. Line a baking sheet with parchment paper.

2   Place the bread in a small bowl, then add a little water to soften it. Let sit for 10 minutes, then squeeze out the excess water.

3   Crumble the tuna into a medium bowl, then add the softened bread, Parmesan, eggs, minced garlic clove, and parsley. Add the Espelette pepper and season with salt and black pepper. Mix well with your hands to form a homogeneous mixture. Shape the tuna mixture into 12 equal-size meatballs, about 1½ inches (4 cm) in diameter, and place them on the prepared baking sheet. Brush the meatballs with the 2 tablespoons oil. Bake for 25 minutes, or until golden brown.

4   **MEANWHILE, MAKE THE TOMATO SAUCE:** In a large skillet, heat the 1 tablespoon oil over medium-high heat. Add the onion, 3 minced garlic cloves, and red pepper flakes and sauté until the onion is translucent. Add the crushed tomatoes, bay leaves, oregano, and pinch of salt and let cook over medium-low heat for 20 to 25 minutes, stirring occasionally.

5   Place the cooked tuna meatballs in the pan with the tomato sauce and cook for an additional 5 minutes. Garnish with curly parsley and serve warm.

Sea Bass with Crispy Chorizo and Sweet Potato Purée

BAR AU CHORIZO CROUSTILLANT
ET PURÉE DE PATATES DOUCES

Here's a fresh and flavorful way to enjoy sea bass. This delicate fish is topped with crispy chorizo for a spicy kick and paired with a rich purée. The contrast of textures and flavors makes this dish a delightful choice for a special dinner, yet it's simple enough to prepare any night of the week.

YIELD 4 SERVINGS
PREP TIME 15 MINUTES
COOK TIME 20 MINUTES

SWEET POTATO AND BROWN BUTTER PUREE

2⅔ pounds (1.2 kg) sweet potatoes, peeled and cut into 1-inch (2.5 cm) cubes

¼ cup (60 g) unsalted butter

¼ cup (60 ml) unsweetened almond milk

1 tablespoon fresh lemon juice (optional)

1 pinch salt

1 pinch ground nutmeg

Black pepper

CRISPY BREAD CRUMBS

½ cup panko (40 g) or regular (50 g) bread crumbs

1 tablespoon olive oil

CRISPY CHORIZO AND OIL

1 chorizo or similar spicy sausage (5 inches, or 12.5 cm, long)

2 tablespoons olive oil

SEA BASS

4 skin-on sea bass fillets

Salt and black pepper

1 tablespoon olive oil

FOR GARNISHING

¼ cup (11 g) finely chopped chives

Black pepper

1 **TO MAKE THE SWEET POTATO AND BROWN BUTTER MASH:** Place the sweet potato cubes in a large saucepan, cover with water, and bring to a boil. Once boiling, reduce the heat to medium-high and cook for 20 to 25 minutes, until tender. Drain.

2 While the sweet potatoes are cooking, melt the butter in a small saucepan over medium-low heat for 6 to 7 minutes, until it starts to brown and develop small brown particles. Pour the brown butter into a small bowl.

---

continued on following page

3   Mash the potatoes using a potato masher. Add the almond milk, lemon juice (if using), pinch of salt, nutmeg, and pepper to taste. Pour the brown butter through a small sieve, to filter the brown particles, into the mashed potatoes. Mix well until the desired consistency is reached.

4   **TO MAKE THE CRISPY BREAD CRUMBS:** Mix the panko and 1 tablespoon oil in a large skillet over medium heat. Toast the panko, stirring regularly, until golden brown. Remove from the skillet.

5   **TO MAKE THE CRISPY CHORIZO AND OIL:** Remove the skin from the chorizo and chop it finely. In the same skillet the bread crumbs were toasted in, heat the 2 tablespoons oil over medium-high heat. Add the chopped chorizo and sauté for 5 to 8 minutes, until crispy. Remove from the pan, along with the orange-colored oil; reserve this oil for serving.

6   **TO MAKE THE SEA BASS:** Season the sea bass fillets with salt and pepper on both sides. Using the same skillet again, heat the 1 tablespoon oil over medium-high heat. When the oil is hot, place the sea bass fillets skin sides down, cooking in batches if necessary to avoid overcrowding the pan. Flatten the fillets with a spatula to prevent them from curling. Let cook for 30 seconds, then reduce the heat to medium and continue cooking for about 3 minutes without moving them. When two-thirds of the sides of the fillets start to turn white and the skin is crispy, flip the fillets and cook for another 1 to 2 minutes, depending on their thickness.

7   Spread some sweet potato puree on the bottom of each plate, add a sea bass fillet, and top with crispy chorizo and a drizzle of reserved chorizo oil. Garnish with crispy bread crumbs, chopped chives, and some pepper.

Baked Salmon with Almond, Olive, and Preserved Lemon Salsa

SAUMON AU FOUR
ET SALSA À L'AMANDE, OLIVE ET CITRON CONFIT

This baked salmon is perfect for a dinner party. You can prepare it in advance and put it in the oven at the last minute. The tangy salsa made with almonds, green olives and homemade preserved lemon adds a unique twist!

1 **TO MAKE THE QUICK PRESERVED LEMON:** Thoroughly wash and dry the lemon. Cut it into quarters and remove any visible seeds.

2 Mix the sea salt and juice of ½ lemon in a small jar until the salt is almost dissolved. Place the lemon quarters in the container, tightly seal it, and shake well to ensure the lemon is coated with the lemon juice. Let it marinate at room temperature for 24 hours. This preserved lemon can be stored for up to 2 weeks in a dark, dry place at room temperature.

3 **TO MAKE THE SALMON:** Preheat the oven to 350°F (180°C) on the convection setting.

4 Season the salmon fillet with salt and pepper on both sides. Line a baking tray with parchment paper and place the fillet on it; if it has skin, place skin side down. Brush the fillet with the 1 tablespoon oil. Bake for 15 to 20 minutes, depending on the thickness of the salmon, until the flesh is pale pink and flakes easily with a fork.

5 **MEANWHILE, MAKE THE ALMOND, GREEN OLIVE, AND PRESERVED LEMON SALSA:** Toast the sliced almonds in a dry skillet (without any oil) over medium-high heat, stirring continuously, until they begin to turn golden brown. Remove them from the pan.

———

continued on following page

YIELD 4 SERVINGS
PREP TIME 15 MINUTES, PLUS 24 HOURS MARINATING
COOK TIME 20 MINUTES

QUICK PRESERVED LEMON (MAKE AT LEAST 24 HOURS IN ADVANCE; SEE NOTES ON PAGE 114)

1 large organic lemon

1½ tablespoons sea salt

Juice of ½ lemon

SALMON

1¾ pounds (800 g) fresh skinless or skin-on whole salmon fillet

Salt and black pepper

1 tablespoon olive oil

ALMOND, GREEN OLIVE, AND PRESERVED LEMON SALSA

½ cup (55 g) sliced almonds

¾ cup (90 g) pitted green olives, drained and chopped

1 or 2 quarters preserved lemon, or more to taste, chopped

¼ cup (13 g) finely chopped flat-leaf parsley

2 tablespoons olive oil

1 tablespoon fresh lemon juice

Salt and black pepper

6   In a medium bowl, mix the olives, chopped preserved
    lemon, parsley, 2 tablespoons oil, and 1 tablespoon lemon
    juice. Season with salt and pepper. (Be cautious not to
    add too much salt, as the olives and preserved lemon are
    naturally salty.)

7   Right before serving, add the toasted almonds to the salsa
    and stir to combine (you want them to be crunchy).

8   Top the salmon with the salsa and serve immediately
    (see Notes).

notes

If you don't have time to make the quick preserved lemon,
mix the grated zest from 1 large lemon with a pinch of salt
and a splash of fresh lemon juice. Let marinate for
30 minutes, then add it to the salsa.

Enjoy this salmon with couscous, bulgur, or rice, such as
the Rice Pilaf with Caramelized Shallots, Dried Apricots,
and Cashews (page 167).

Tuna Steak with Tomato, Olives, and Capers

STEAK DE THON
AUX TOMATES, OLIVES ET CÂPRES

This is one of my favorite dishes to make with white tuna steak. It's ideal to make for a quick weekday meal or an easy fancy dinner. The tangy tomato and balsamic vinegar sauce perfectly complements the subtle flavors of the fish.

1 Season the tuna steaks with salt and pepper on both sides.

2 In a large skillet, heat 1 tablespoon of the oil over medium-high heat. Add the tuna steaks and sear for 1 minute per side; the steaks should not be cooked through. Remove the steaks from the pan.

3 To the same skillet, add the remaining 1 tablespoon oil and the onion over medium-high heat and sauté until the onion is translucent. Add the garlic, chili pepper, and tomato paste and sauté for 1 minute.

4 Pour in the balsamic vinegar and deglaze by scraping the bottom of the pan with a wooden spoon to release any browned bits. Add the tomatoes and bay leaves and season with salt and pepper. Let simmer over a medium-low heat for 10 to 15 minutes, until the sauce has thickened. At the end of cooking, add the capers and olives, then return the tuna steaks to the skillet and let cook for another 5 to 10 minutes, until the fish flakes easily with a fork.

5 Garnish with the chopped parsley and serve immediately (see Notes).

———

notes Try this recipe with other fish, such as cod, halibut, or swordfish—swordfish is my favorite alternative.

Serve this dish with pasta or rice to soak up the delicious sauce.

YIELD 2 PORTIONS
PREP TIME 10 MINUTES
COOK TIME 20 MINUTES

2 white tuna steaks (see Notes)

Salt and black pepper

2 tablespoons olive oil, divided

1 medium red onion, thinly sliced

2 cloves garlic, minced

1 mild fresh chili pepper, diced

1 tablespoon tomato paste

2 tablespoons balsamic vinegar

1 can (14 ounces, or 400 g) diced tomatoes

2 bay leaves

2 tablespoons capers, drained

½ cup (60 g) pitted black olives

¼ cup (13 g) finely chopped flat-leaf parsley, for garnishing

Salmon and Leek Quiche

QUICHE AU SAUMON
ET AUX POIREAUX

This quiche is perfect for a light lunch or a cozy dinner. Encased in a buttery, flaky homemade shortcrust pastry, the salmon in the filling pairs beautifully with the tender sautéed leeks and hint of dill.

YIELD 6 SERVINGS
PREP TIME 15 MINUTES
COOK TIME 55 MINUTES

2 tablespoons unsalted butter, plus more for greasing

4 medium leeks, washed and cut into thin slices

Salt and black pepper

1 chilled ball Shortcrust Pastry without Egg (page 14)

All-purpose flour, for dusting

4 medium eggs

½ cup (120 ml) heavy whipping cream

½ cup (25 g) chopped fresh dill (see Note)

1 pinch ground nutmeg

14 ounces (400 g) fresh skinless salmon fillets (see Note), cut into 1-inch (2.5 cm) cubes

1 In a large skillet, melt the 2 tablespoons butter over medium heat. Add the leeks and sauté for 10 minutes, or until slightly tender. Season with salt and pepper and remove from the heat.

2 Preheat the oven to 350°F (180°C) on the convection setting. Line an 11-inch (28 cm) tart pan with parchment paper or grease it with butter.

3 Place the chilled dough ball on a floured surface and roll it out with a rolling pin into a circle at least 2 inches (5 cm) larger in diameter than the tart pan. Transfer the dough to the prepared pan. Trim off any excess dough from the edges. Prick the base of the dough with a fork. Lay a sheet of parchment paper over the dough and fill it with pie weights, dried beans, or uncooked rice. Blind-bake it for 10 to 15 minutes, until the edges start to harden. Remove from the oven, leaving the oven on.

4 Meanwhile, whisk together the eggs with the cream and dill in a medium bowl. Add the nutmeg and season with salt and pepper.

5 Spread the salmon cubes over the prebaked crust. Add the leeks, then pour the egg mixture over the top. Bake for 35 to 40 minutes, until the filling is firm and the crust is golden brown. If the quiche starts to blacken while baking, cover it with aluminum foil. Let cool for 5 minutes, then slice and serve.

note
You can also prepare this quiche using smoked salmon or a combination of both fresh and smoked salmon. If you don't like dill, replace it with chopped chives or parsley.

VEGETARIAN MAINS

Omelet with Green Onions and Comté

OMELETTE
AUX CÉBETTES ET AU COMTÉ

This omelet is a delightful specialty from the south of France and is perfect for a quick, simple, and budget-friendly meal. Enjoy with a green salad.

YIELD 2 SERVINGS
PREP TIME 5 MINUTES
COOK TIME 15 MINUTES

2 tablespoons olive oil, divided

6 green onions, cut into
½-inch-thick (1.5 cm) slices

6 large eggs

⅓ cup (35 g) grated Comté
or Gruyère cheese

Salt and black pepper

1 pinch Espelette pepper
(or use less cayenne pepper)

Fleur de sel or sea salt flakes,
for garnishing

1 In a medium skillet, heat 1 tablespoon of the oil over medium heat. Add the green onions and sauté for 3 to 5 minutes, until they start to soften. If they start to brown too quickly, add a few drops of water to prevent burning.

2 While the onions are cooking, beat the eggs in a large bowl. Stir in the cheese and season with salt and black pepper. Add the Espelette pepper. Mix in the sautéed green onions.

3 Preheat the oven on the broiler setting.

4 Heat the remaining 1 tablespoon oil in the same skillet over medium heat. Add the egg-onion mixture and cook for 3 to 5 minutes, until the edges start to set. Gently loosen the edges of the omelet with a spatula. Once the omelet begins to set, place it under the broiler for 2 to 3 minutes to lightly brown the top.

5 Sprinkle with fleur de sel. Serve warm.

TARTE TATIN AUX TOMATES

This tomato tarte tatin is a fresh twist on the Classic Apple Tarte Tatin (page 191). Juicy tomatoes, seasoned with thyme and balsamic vinegar, are cooked upside down in flaky puff pastry. It's an impressive yet simple dish, perfect for a light summer meal or an elegant starter.

1   Preheat the oven to 350°F (180°C) on the convection setting.

2   Season the cut sides of the tomato halves with salt and pepper, then sprinkle with the herbes de Provence and garlic powder.

3   In a large skillet, heat the oil over medium heat. Carefully place the tomatoes in the skillet, cut sides down, and sear for about 2 minutes, or until they begin to caramelize. Pour the balsamic vinegar over the tomatoes and let it reduce over medium-low heat for 5 to 10 minutes, ensuring that it thickens slightly without moving the tomatoes.

4   Transfer the tomatoes to an 11-inch (28 cm) tart pan, placing them cut sides up and packing them tightly. Pour any remaining juices from the skillet over the tomatoes.

5   Cover the tomatoes with the puff pastry, tucking the edges in to securely encase the filling. Gently prick the dough with a fork to let the air escape during baking. Bake for about 35 minutes, or until the puff pastry is golden brown. Carefully remove the tart from the oven, then run a knife alongside the edges of the tart pan to release the puff pastry. Place a plate over the top of the tart, then swiftly invert the pan to flip the tart onto the plate. Serve warm garnished with thyme leaves (if using) (see Note).

---

note   Sprinkle with crumbled fresh goat or feta cheese right before serving for extra flavor.

YIELD 6 SERVINGS
PREP TIME 15 MINUTES
COOK TIME 45 MINUTES

1⅔ pounds (750 g) small tomatoes (such as Roma or plum), cut in half crosswise

Salt and black pepper

1 tablespoon Herbes de Provence (page 11)

1 teaspoon garlic powder

2 tablespoons olive oil

2 tablespoons balsamic vinegar

1 sheet frozen puff pastry, thawed

Fresh thyme leaves, for garnishing (optional)

Penne alla Pastis

PENNE AU PASTIS

If you're short on cooking time but craving an elegant pasta meal, this recipe, inspired by the famous Italian pasta alla vodka, is perfect. Pastis, an anise-flavored liqueur from the south of France, adds a subtle note that truly enhances the flavor of this cream and tomato–based sauce.

YIELD 2 SERVINGS
PREP TIME 10 MINUTES
COOK TIME 20 MINUTES

Salt

9 ounces (250 g) pasta of choice

2 tablespoons olive oil

1 medium shallot, finely chopped

2 cloves garlic, minced

3 tablespoons tomato paste

1 pinch Espelette pepper (or use less cayenne pepper)

Black pepper

1 can (14 ounces, or 400 g) whole peeled or crushed tomatoes

¼ cup (60 ml) pastis (see Note)

½ cup (120 ml) heavy whipping cream

¼ cup (30 g) grated Parmesan cheese, plus more for garnishing

Finely chopped fresh flat-leaf parsley, for garnishing

1 Bring a large pot of salted water to a boil. Once the water is boiling, add the pasta and cook to al dente according to the package instructions. Before draining, reserve ¼ cup (60 ml) of the pasta cooking water.

2 Meanwhile, heat the oil in a large skillet over medium-high heat. Add the shallot and sauté for about 3 minutes, or until translucent. Add the garlic and sauté for 2 more minutes. Stir in the tomato paste, then add the Espelette pepper and season with salt and black pepper. Cook for about 2 minutes, stirring to combine well.

3 Pour in the can of tomatoes and let simmer over medium-low heat for 10 to 15 minutes, stirring regularly, until the sauce has thickened. (Optionally, you can now transfer the sauce to a blender and blend to obtain a smooth tomato sauce, then pour it back into the skillet.)

4 Add the pastis and cook for 3 minutes over medium-high heat to allow the alcohol to evaporate. Reduce the heat to medium-low, then add the cream, stirring to combine well.

5 Add the cooked pasta to the skillet along with the reserved pasta water to thicken the sauce and mix well. Finish by stirring in the Parmesan.

6 Divide the pasta between the plates and garnish with more Parmesan and chopped parsley. Serve immediately.

———

note If you don't have pastis but want the same anise flavor, add 1 star anise to the sauce with the tomatoes in step 3. Let it infuse until the sauce thickens, then remove and discard it before serving.

Vegetarian Lentil and Eggplant Parmentier

PARMENTIER VÉGÉTARIEN
AU LENTILLES ET AUBERGINE

Hachis parmentier, a staple in French cuisine, usually features minced duck meat. However, this vegetarian version with lentils and eggplant surpasses it, in my opinion. It's a versatile and convenient dish, which is ideal for prepping meals for the week ahead.

YIELD 6 SERVINGS
PREP TIME 30 MINUTES
COOK TIME 1 HOUR

LENTIL AND EGGPLANT FILLING

2 tablespoons olive oil, plus more if needed

1 large eggplant (about 9 ounces, or 250 g), cut into ½-inch (1.5 cm) cubes

Salt and black pepper

2 medium yellow onions, finely chopped

2 medium carrots (about 10 ounces, or 300 g), cut into ¼-inch (6 mm) dice

2 celery ribs, cut into ¼-inch (6 mm) dice

3 cloves garlic, minced

3 tablespoons tomato paste

1 teaspoon red pepper flakes

¼ cup (60 ml) dry red wine

2¾ cups (660 ml) vegetable broth

1 can (14 ounces, or 400 g) diced or whole peeled tomatoes

1 cup (200 g) dried French green lentils

2 bay leaves

2 tablespoons dried thyme

MASHED POTATOES

2¼ pounds (1 kg) starchy potatoes (such as russet or Yukon Gold), peeled and cut into large pieces

1 tablespoon coarse salt

¾ cup (180 ml) whole milk

¼ cup (60 g) unsalted butter, or more to taste, plus more for greasing

Salt and black pepper

¼ teaspoon ground nutmeg

¼ cup (25 g) bread crumbs

1 **TO MAKE THE LENTIL AND EGGPLANT FILLING:** In a large, deep skillet, heat the oil over medium heat. Add the eggplant and sauté for 5 minutes, or until it begins to turn golden. Add a few drops of water if it starts to stick to the pan. Season with salt and pepper and remove from the skillet.

———

continued on following page

2   In the same skillet, add the onions, carrots, and celery and sauté until the onion is translucent. Add a little oil if needed. Add the garlic, cooked eggplant, tomato paste, and red pepper flakes and sauté for 2 minutes.

3   Pour in the red wine and deglaze the pan by scraping the bottom of the pan with a wooden spoon to release any browned bits. Let the wine reduce slightly, then add the broth, tomatoes, and lentils. Season with salt and pepper and add the bay leaves and thyme. Let simmer for 30 to 35 minutes, until the lentils are tender. Remove and discard the bay leaves.

4   **MEANWHILE, MAKE THE MASHED POTATOES:** Fill a large pot with cold water, then add the potato pieces. Bring to a boil, add the coarse salt, and let cook for 25 to 30 minutes, until the potatoes are fork-tender.

5   In a small saucepan, heat the milk and butter over low heat until the butter melts. Remove the pan from the heat.

6   Preheat the oven to 390°F (200°C) on the convection setting. Grease an 11 x 9-inch (28 x 23 cm) baking dish with butter.

7   Drain the potatoes and mash them with a potato masher. Gradually pour in the milk-butter mixture, mixing well to incorporate it into the potatoes. Season with salt and pepper and the nutmeg.

8   Pour the lentil and eggplant filling into the prepared baking dish. Top with the mashed potatoes, evenly spreading them over the filling, then sprinkle the mashed potatoes with the bread crumbs.

9   Bake for 30 to 35 minutes, until the top is golden brown. Serve warm.

———

note   You can vary this recipe by using the Olive Oil and Lemon Mashed Potatoes (page 156), which will also make this dish vegan.

QUICHE AUX BLETTES ET AUX CHAMPIGNONS
À LA PÂTE BRISÉE DE SARRASIN

This recipe is a simple way to prepare Swiss chard in the fall. Buckwheat flour gives the shortcrust pastry a nutty flavor that blends perfectly with the mushrooms and red onion.

1   **TO MAKE THE BUCKWHEAT SHORTCRUST PASTRY:** In a large bowl, combine the flours and ½ teaspoon salt. Add the 3 tablespoons oil, the egg, and the cold water. Mix until the dough comes together. (If the dough is too dry, add a bit more water; buckwheat flour tends to absorb water.) Shape the dough into a ball, wrap it in plastic wrap, and refrigerate for at least 30 minutes.

2   Preheat the oven to 350°F (180°C) on the convection setting. Grease an 11-inch (28 cm) tart pan with oil or butter.

3   **MEANWHILE, MAKE THE FILLING:** In a large skillet, heat the 1 tablespoon oil over medium heat. Add the mushrooms and sauté for 2 minutes. Add the garlic and continue cooking until the mushrooms are softened and any liquid they release has evaporated. Stir in the Swiss chard and cook until wilted. Season with salt and pepper. Remove the pan from the heat.

———

continued on following page

YIELD 4 SERVINGS
PREP TIME 20 MINUTES, PLUS 30 MINUTES CHILLING
COOK TIME 40 MINUTES

BUCKWHEAT SHORTCRUST PASTRY

1 cup (120 g) all-purpose flour

½ cup (60 g) buckwheat flour

½ teaspoon salt

3 tablespoons olive oil, plus more for greasing (optional)

1 medium egg

¼ cup (60 ml) cold water, plus more if needed

Unsalted butter, for greasing (optional)

FILLING

1 tablespoon olive oil

2 cups (140 g) sliced button mushrooms

2 cloves garlic, minced

1 pound (455 g) Swiss chard (see Note on page 132), stems removed and leaves chopped into bite-size pieces

Salt and black pepper

4 large eggs

⅔ cup (160 ml) heavy whipping cream

½ large red onion, thinly sliced

½ cup (50 g) whole walnuts, roughly chopped

4 Place the chilled dough ball on a floured surface and roll it out with a rolling pin into a circle at least 2 inches (5 cm) larger in diameter than the tart pan. Transfer the dough to the prepared pan. Trim off any excess dough from the edges. Prick the base of the dough with a fork. Lay a sheet of parchment paper over the dough and fill it with pie weights, dried beans, or uncooked rice. Blind-bake it for 10 to 15 minutes, until the edges start to harden. Remove from the oven, leaving the oven on.

5 In a medium bowl, whisk together the eggs and cream with salt and pepper.

6 Spread the sautéed chard-mushroom mixture over the prebaked crust. Add the onion slices and walnuts, then pour the egg mixture over the top.

7 Bake for 25 to 30 minutes, until the filling is set and the crust is golden brown. Let cool slightly before slicing and serving.

———

note You can make this quiche with fresh or frozen spinach instead of Swiss chard. If you're using frozen spinach, first thaw it in the microwave, then squeeze out the excess water.

Zucchini Waffles with Buckwheat Flour

GAUFRES DE COURGETTES
À LA FARINE DE SARRASIN

I love making these savory waffles for breakfast or for a quick, healthy weekday meal. They are made with buckwheat flour, which makes them naturally gluten-free. Their texture is perfect—crispy on the outside and soft on the inside!

1   Trim off the ends of the zucchini and grate them using a grater or food processor. (If they release water, it's okay; it will help moisten the batter.)

2   In a large bowl, combine the flour, cornstarch, milk, cheese, eggs, baking powder, coriander, Espelette pepper, and salt and black pepper to taste. Add the grated zucchini and mix until the zucchini is well incorporated into the batter. (The batter may seem dense initially, but as you work it, the zucchini will release more water, resulting in a thinner batter.) Let the batter rest for 15 minutes.

3   Preheat a waffle iron and lightly grease the plates with oil to prevent sticking. Pour ⅔ cup (160 ml) of batter onto the iron and cook for 8 to 10 minutes, until the waffle is golden brown and crispy on the outside. Repeat with the remaining batter. (If you don't have a waffle iron, heat some oil in a large skillet over medium-high heat. Drop 1 to 3 ladlefuls—about ⅔ cup, or 160 ml, per ladle—of batter into the pan to form thick pancakes and cook for 4 to 5 minutes per side. Repeat with the remaining batter.) Serve immediately (see Note)

note   Serve these waffles with some lettuce leaves, an egg, and the Creamy Chive Dip (page 143) for a quick meal. Or pair it with the Roasted Tomato and Bell Pepper Soup (page 51) or the Crouton and Tomato Salad with Lemon-Anchovy Vinaigrette (page 62).

YIELD 4 TO 6 WAFFLES
PREP TIME 15 MINUTES, PLUS 15 MINUTES RESTING
COOK TIME 35 MINUTES

2 zucchini (1 pound, or 455 g)

1 cup (120 g) buckwheat flour

½ cup (60 g) cornstarch

¼ cup (60 ml) whole milk

1 cup (100 g) grated Swiss cheese (such as Emmental or Gruyère)

2 large eggs

½ teaspoon baking powder

½ teaspoon ground coriander

1 pinch Espelette pepper (or use less cayenne pepper)

Salt and black pepper

Olive oil, for greasing

Vegetable Quiche Tian-Style

QUICHE AUX LÉGUMES FAÇON TIAN

A tian is a traditional Provençal dish featuring colorfully arranged, oven-baked vegetables, and should not be mistaken for ratatouille (page XX). This is a creative twist on the classic recipe.

YIELD 6 SERVINGS
PREP TIME 15 MINUTES
COOK TIME 45 MINUTES

Unsalted butter, for greasing (optional)

1 chilled ball Shortcrust Pastry with Whole Egg (page 13) (Note: Add 1 tablespoon dried thyme when mixing the flour, butter, and salt)

All-purpose flour, for dusting

1 medium zucchini, thinly sliced into rounds

1 medium yellow squash, thinly sliced into rounds

2 tablespoons olive oil

2 tablespoons Herbes de Provence (page 11)

Salt and black pepper

3 medium eggs

¼ cup (60 ml) heavy whipping cream

½ cup (60 g) grated Parmesan cheese

2 cloves garlic, minced

1 pinch Espelette pepper (or use less cayenne pepper)

3 large red onions, thinly sliced into half-moons

4 medium tomatoes, thinly sliced into rounds

Basil leaves, for garnishing

1 Preheat the oven to 350°F (180°C) on the convection setting. Line an 11-inch (28 cm) tart pan with parchment paper or grease it with butter.

2 Place the chilled dough ball on a floured surface and roll it out with a rolling pin into a circle at least 2 inches (5 cm) larger in diameter than the tart pan. Transfer the dough to the prepared pan. Trim off any excess dough from the edges. Prick the base of the dough with a fork. Lay a sheet of parchment paper over the dough and fill it with pie weights, dried beans, or uncooked rice. Blind-bake it for 10 to 15 minutes, until the edges start to harden. Remove from the oven, leaving the oven on.

3 Meanwhile, in a large bowl, toss the zucchini and squash with the olive oil, herbes de Provence, and salt and black pepper to taste to thoroughly coat the vegetables.

4 In a medium bowl, whisk together the eggs, cream, Parmesan, garlic, salt and black pepper to taste, and Espelette pepper.

5 Pour the egg mixture into the prebaked crust. Arrange the vegetable slices on the crust, alternating zucchini, onion, squash, and tomato, layering from the outside inward until covered. Season again with salt and black pepper. Bake for 35 to 40 minutes, until the vegetables are tender and the crust is golden brown. Let cool for 5 minutes. Garnish with basil leaves, then slice and serve.

CRUMBLE D'AVOINE
À LA BUTTERNUT, FETA ET NOIX

Savory crumbles are very popular in France, as it's an original way to roast vegetables and give them some crunch. This crumble, made with rolled oats, is very healthy, and I really like this combination of butternut squash, feta cheese, and walnuts.

1   Preheat the oven to 390°F (200°C) on the convection setting.

2   **TO MAKE THE VEGETABLES:** Place the squash, zucchini, garlic, and thyme in an 11-inch (28 cm) oval baking dish. Season with salt and black pepper, then add the Espelette pepper. Drizzle the oil over the vegetables and mix well to coat all the vegetables.

3   Bake for 20 minutes, or until the vegetables start to caramelize. Remove from the oven, leaving the oven on.

4   **MEANWHILE, MAKE THE OAT CRUMBLE:** Add the oats to a blender and pulse to get a coarse powder, leaving some larger pieces for texture.

5   In a medium bowl, mix the pulsed oats with the butter and salt, using your fingers, until you get a crumbly texture. Add the feta to the oat mixture, leaving some chunks.

6   Sprinkle the feta over the vegetables, add the walnuts, and mix well. Spread the oat crumble over the vegetables and bake for another 25 minutes, or until the crumble is golden brown. Serve immediately (see Note).

note   You can serve this dish as a main course with a green salad or as a side, pairing it with the Creamy Tarragon and Mushroom Chicken (page 98) or the Marinated Pork Chops with Herbes de Provence (page 94).

YIELD 4 TO 6 SERVINGS
PREP TIME 20 MINUTES
COOK TIME 45 MINUTES

VEGETABLES

2¼ pounds (1 kg) butternut squash, peeled, seeds removed, and cut into ¾-inch cubes

1 large zucchini (about 12 ounces, or 340 g), cut in half lengthwise, then thinly sliced into half-moons

2 cloves garlic, minced

2 tablespoons dried thyme

Salt and black pepper

1 pinch Espelette pepper (or use less cayenne pepper)

3 tablespoons olive oil

½ cup (75 g) crumbled feta cheese

⅔ cup (65 g) whole walnuts, roughly chopped

OAT CRUMBLE

2½ cups (200 g) rolled oats

½ cup (120 g) unsalted butter

1 pinch salt

½ cup (75 g) crumbled feta cheese

Spring Quiche with Asparagus, Broccoli, and Peas

QUICHE DE PRINTEMPS
AUX ASPERGES, BROCOLI ET PETITS POIS

You will love how the fresh flavors of spring vegetables blend with the creamy goat cheese. Serve this quiche with a green salad or the Crouton and Tomato Salad with Lemon-Anchovy Vinaigrette (page 62) for a light meal.

YIELD 6 SERVINGS
PREP TIME 20 MINUTES,
PLUS 15 MINUTES CHILLING
COOK TIME 45 MINUTES

Unsalted butter, for greasing (optional)

1 chilled ball Shortcrust Pastry with Whole Egg (page 13)

All-purpose flour, for dusting

Salt

1 small head broccoli, trimmed and separated into florets

4 medium eggs

½ cup (120 ml) heavy whipping cream

½ cup (120 ml) whole milk

1 clove garlic, minced

Black pepper

10 medium green asparagus stalks, trimmed, stems sliced into 2-inch (5 cm) pieces, and heads left intact

1 cup (135 g) frozen peas

2 green onions, thinly sliced, plus more for garnishing

5 ounces (150 g) fresh goat cheese, crumbled

1 Preheat the oven to 350°F (180°C) on the convection setting. Line an 11-inch (28 cm) tart pan with parchment paper or grease it with butter.

2 Place the chilled dough ball on a floured surface and roll it out with a rolling pin into a circle at least 2 inches (5 cm) larger in diameter than the tart pan. Transfer the dough to the prepared pan. Trim off any excess dough from the edges. Prick the base of the dough with a fork. Lay a sheet of parchment paper over the dough and fill it with pie weights, dried beans, or uncooked rice. Blind-bake it for 10 to 15 minutes, until the edges start to harden. Remove from the oven, leaving the oven on.

3 Meanwhile, bring a large pot of salted water to a boil. Optionally, prepare a large bowl with cold water and ice for an ice bath. Once the water is boiling, add the broccoli. Blanch it for 3 minutes, then drain. If using, transfer the broccoli to the ice bath for 3 minutes to help keep its bright green color.

4 In a medium bowl, whisk together the eggs, cream, milk, garlic, and salt and pepper to taste.

5 Spread the blanched broccoli, asparagus pieces, peas, and green onion slices over the prebaked crust. Sprinkle the crumbled goat cheese over the vegetables, then evenly pour the egg mixture over the top.

6 Bake for 30 to 35 minutes, until the filling is set and the crust is golden brown. Let cool for a few minutes, then garnish with green onion slices. Slice and serve warm.

Crispy Smashed Potatoes with Fennel Salad

POMMES DE TERRE ÉCRASÉES
AVEC SALADE DE FENOUIL

This recipe has become one of my staples. I often serve it with a creamy chive dip and a salad—in this case, one made with thinly sliced fennel and cucumber.

1 **TO MAKE THE CRISPY SMASHED POTATOES:** Preheat the oven to 390°F (200°C) on the convection setting. Line a baking sheet with parchment paper or a silicone baking mat.

2 Salt a large pot of cold water, then add the potatoes and bring to a boil. Once boiling, reduce the heat to medium and cook the potatoes for 25 minutes, or until fork-tender. Drain.

3 Meanwhile, mix the ¼ cup (60 ml) oil, garlic powder, paprika, ½ teaspoon salt, and pepper to taste in a small bowl until well combined. Spread the boiled potatoes on the prepared baking sheet in a single layer. Using the bottom of a glass, slightly flatten the potatoes, then brush them with the oil mixture. Bake for 25 to 30 minutes, until golden brown.

4 **TO MAKE THE FENNEL AND CUCUMBER SALAD:** Remove the hard end of the fennel bulb, then cut the bulb in half. Using a mandoline, carefully slice the fennel and cucumber very thinly. Add the fennel, cucumber, fleur de sel, grated lemon zest, 3 tablespoons lemon juice, 3 tablespoons oil, and parsley to a medium bowl. Mix well.

5 **TO MAKE THE CREAMY CHIVE DIP:** In a small bowl, mix the yogurt, crème fraîche, 1 tablespoon lemon juice, and chives. Season with sea salt and pepper.

6 Serve the warm smashed potatoes with the creamy chive dip and fennel and cucumber salad.

YIELD 4 SERVINGS
PREP TIME 10 MINUTES
COOK TIME 50 MINUTES

CRISPY SMASHED POTATOES

½ teaspoon salt, plus more for cooking water

1 pound (455 g) baby potatoes, cut in half

¼ cup (60 ml) olive oil

½ teaspoon garlic powder

½ teaspoon paprika

Black pepper

FENNEL AND CUCUMBER SALAD

1 large fennel bulb

½ English cucumber

1 pinch fleur de sel or sea salt flakes

1 medium lemon, for zesting and juicing

3 tablespoons olive oil

¼ cup (9 g) finely chopped fresh curly parsley

CREAMY CHIVE DIP

⅔ cup (160 g) plain Greek yogurt

⅓ cup (80 g) crème fraîche or sour cream

1 tablespoon fresh lemon juice

¼ cup (11 g) finely chopped fresh chives

Sea salt and black pepper

Arugula, Cherry Tomato, and Feta Quiche

QUICHE À LA ROQUETTE
AUX TOMATES CERISES ET À LA FETA

Have you ever had cooked arugula? This quiche is a great way to try it, where it goes well with the creaminess of the feta cheese and cherry tomatoes. To make this quiche light, I used my recipe for yogurt shortcrust pastry, without butter or oil!

YIELD 6 SERVINGS
PREP TIME 10 MINUTES
COOK TIME 40 MINUTES

Unsalted butter, for greasing (optional)

2 tablespoons olive oil, plus more for greasing (optional)

1 chilled ball Yogurt Shortcrust Pastry (page 14)

All-purpose flour, for dusting

5 cups (100 g) arugula (or substitute with fresh baby spinach)

Salt and black pepper

2 cups (200 g) cherry tomatoes, cut in half crosswise

1¼ cups (200 g) crumbled feta cheese

4 medium eggs

1 cup (240 ml) heavy whipping cream

2 cloves garlic, minced

1 pinch Espelette pepper

1   Preheat the oven to 350°F (180°C) on the convection setting. Grease an 11-inch (28 cm) tart pan with butter.

2   Place the chilled dough ball on a floured surface and roll it out with a rolling pin into a circle at least 2 inches (5 cm) larger in diameter than the tart pan. Transfer the dough to the prepared pan. Trim off any excess dough from the edges. Prick the base of the dough with a fork. Lay a sheet of parchment paper over the dough and fill it with pie weights, dried beans, or uncooked rice. Blind-bake it for 10 minutes, or until the edges start to harden. Remove from the oven, leaving the oven on.

3   Meanwhile, heat the 2 tablespoons oil in a medium skillet over medium heat. Add the arugula and sauté for 3 minutes, or until slightly wilted. Season with salt and black pepper. Spread the cooked arugula over the prebaked crust, then spread the tomatoes, followed by the feta sprinkled on top.

4   In a small bowl, whisk together the eggs and cream with the garlic, Espelette pepper, and salt and black pepper to taste. Pour the egg mixture over the vegetables and cheese in the pan. Bake for 25 to 30 minutes, until the filling is set and the crust is golden brown (see Note).

note   The yogurt shortcrust pastry is crispier and bakes a bit faster than a traditional shortcrust. If you're using this crust with a different filling, ensure the filling doesn't require a long cook time.

Thin Tart with Artichokes, Ricotta, and Lemon

TARTE FINE

AUX ARTICHAUTS, RICOTTA ET CITRON

Inspired by the flammekueche from Alsace, I have given this thin tart a complete makeover to transform it into a delightful Mediterranean dish. It's easy to prepare, quick to bake, and perfect as an appetizer or a healthy meal when paired with a salad.

1 **TO MAKE THE TART DOUGH:** In a large bowl, combine the flour, 2 tablespoons oil, and ½ teaspoon salt. Add the cold water and mix until a smooth dough forms. Shape the dough into a ball, wrap it in plastic wrap, and refrigerate for at least 30 minutes.

2 Preheat the oven to 400°F (200°C) on the convection setting.

3 Place the chilled dough on a lightly floured surface and roll it out using a rolling pin into a 14 x 10-inch (35 x 25 cm) rectangle. Place the dough on a sheet of parchment paper, then transfer it to a large baking sheet.

4 **TO PREPARE THE TOPPINGS:** In a small bowl, mix the ricotta, garlic, basil, grated lemon zest, 2 tablespoons lemon juice, and salt and pepper to taste until well combined. Spread the ricotta mixture evenly over the dough.

5 Spread the artichokes, mushrooms, and onion over the ricotta. Drizzle with the 1 tablespoon oil and lemon juice and sprinkle with the oregano. Season with salt and pepper.

6 Bake for 15 to 18 minutes, until the crust is golden brown and crispy. Remove from the oven and top with the arugula and olives. Serve immediately.

———

notes

For a traditional Alsatian version, spread crème fraîche or sour cream over the dough, then top it with pan-fried lardons (bacon) and a little chopped yellow onion.

You can easily adapt this recipe with ingredients you have on hand.

YIELD 2 SERVINGS
PREP TIME 10 MINUTES, PLUS 30 MINUTES CHILLING
COOK TIME 15 MINUTES

TART DOUGH

2 cups plus 1 tablespoon (250 g) all-purpose flour, plus more for dusting

2 tablespoons olive oil

½ teaspoon salt

½ cup (120 ml) cold water

TOPPINGS

¾ cup (185 g) ricotta cheese

1 clove garlic, minced

⅓ cup (15 g) chopped fresh basil

1 medium lemon, for zesting, juicing, and drizzling, divided

Salt and black pepper

½ cup (120 g) canned or jarred artichoke hearts, drained and cut into quarters

¼ cup (20 g) thinly sliced button mushrooms

¼ medium red onion, thinly sliced

1 tablespoon olive oil

1 tablespoon dried oregano

1 cup (20 g) arugula

2 tablespoons pitted black olives

Pasta with Caramelized Onions, Mushrooms, and Spinach

PÂTES AUX OIGNONS
CARAMÉLISÉS, CHAMPIGNONS ET ÉPINARDS

This is a quick recipe for a weeknight meal. The caramelized onions add a rich sweetness that pairs perfectly with the earthy mushrooms and fresh spinach.

YIELD 2 OR 3 SERVINGS
PREP TIME 10 MINUTES
COOK TIME 30 MINUTES

Salt

7 ounces (200 g) pasta shape of choice (such as fusilli, penne, or orecchiette)

2 tablespoons olive oil, divided

9 ounces (250 g) button mushrooms, thinly sliced

Black pepper

2 medium yellow onions, thinly sliced

2 tablespoons balsamic vinegar

1 tablespoon fresh thyme leaves, plus more for garnishing

1 tablespoon all-purpose flour

¼ cup (60 ml) dry white wine

1 cup (240 ml) vegetable broth

3 cups (90 g) baby spinach or chopped spinach leaves

⅓ cup (40 g) grated Parmesan cheese

Crispy Bread Crumbs (page 37), for garnishing

1   Bring a large pot of salted water to a boil. Once the water is boiling, add the pasta and cook to al dente according to the package instructions. Before draining, reserve ¼ cup (60 ml) of the pasta cooking water.

2   Meanwhile, heat 1 tablespoon of the oil in a large, deep skillet over medium heat. Add the mushrooms and sauté for 5 to 10 minutes, until they are tender and browned. Season with salt and pepper and remove from the pan.

3   To the same skillet, add the remaining 1 tablespoon oil and the onions. Sauté over medium-high heat for 15 to 20 minutes, until they are golden brown, seasoning them with salt and pepper halfway through. (If the onions stick to the skillet, add 1 tablespoon of cold water and stir to deglaze the pan with a wooden spoon, scraping up any browned bits. Repeat if needed.) Toward the end of the cooking time, add the vinegar and thyme. Sprinkle with the flour, stir, and then pour in the wine, scraping up any browned bits. Add the broth and simmer over medium-low heat until thickened.

4   Right before serving, add the cooked pasta, sautéed mushrooms, spinach, Parmesan, and reserved pasta water to the skillet. Cook and stir for a couple of minutes until all the ingredients are well combined. Garnish with more thyme leaves and crispy bread crumbs. Serve immediately.

Zucchini, Mint, and Ricotta Quiche

QUICHE AUX COURGETTES
À LA MENTHE ET À LA RICOTTA

This is a Mediterranean-style quiche with an olive oil crust and an ultra-creamy ricotta filling. As you may notice with some other recipes, I love the combination of zucchini, peas, and mint.

1   Preheat the oven to 350°F (180°C) on the convection setting. Grease an 11-inch (28 cm) tart pan with butter.

2   Place the chilled dough ball on a floured surface and roll it out with a rolling pin into a circle at least 2 inches (5 cm) larger in diameter than the tart pan. Transfer the dough to the pan. Trim off any excess dough from the edges. Prick the base of the dough with a fork. Lay a sheet of parchment paper over the dough and fill it with pie weights, dried beans, or uncooked rice. Blind-bake it for 10 minutes, or until the edges start to harden. Remove from the oven, leaving the oven on.

3   Meanwhile, whisk together the eggs, then add the ricotta, cream, and Parmesan and whisk until smooth. Stir in the garlic, mint, basil, grated lemon zest, and juice from half of the lemon. Season with salt and pepper.

4   Thinly slice the zucchini lengthwise using a mandoline. Spread the zucchini slices and peas over the prebaked crust, then pour the egg-ricotta mixture over the top.

5   Bake for 35 to 40 minutes, until the filling is set and the crust is golden brown. Let cool slightly before slicing and serving.

YIELD 6 SERVINGS
PREP TIME 10 MINUTES
COOK TIME 45 MINUTES

Unsalted butter or olive oil, for greasing

1 chilled ball Olive Oil Shortcrust Pastry (page 14)

All-purpose flour, for dusting

3 medium eggs

1 cup (250 g) ricotta cheese

¼ cup (60 ml) heavy whipping cream

⅔ cup (80 g) grated Parmesan cheese

2 cloves garlic, minced

½ cup (25 g) finely chopped fresh mint

½ cup (20 g) finely chopped fresh basil

1 medium lemon, for zesting and juicing

Salt and black pepper

2 small zucchini

1 cup (135 g) frozen peas

STEAKS DE CHOU-FLEUR
AVEC UN SAUCE AUX OLIVES, AU CITRON ET AU PERSIL

YIELD 2 SERVINGS
PREP TIME 15 MINUTES
COOK TIME 30 MINUTES

CAULIFLOWER STEAKS

1 large head cauliflower

3 tablespoons olive oil

½ teaspoon smoked paprika

½ teaspoon paprika

½ teaspoon garlic powder

Salt and black pepper

CAULIFLOWER PURÉE

1 clove garlic, peeled

3 tablespoons crème fraîche or sour cream

1 tablespoon unsalted butter

Salt

OLIVE, LEMON, AND PARSLEY DIP

¼ cup (30 g) roughly chopped pitted green olives

¼ cup (13 g) finely chopped flat-leaf parsley

1 lemon, for zesting

1 tablespoon fresh lemon juice

¼ cup (60 ml) olive oil

Salt

FOR GARNISHING

Black pepper

Pitted green olives

This elegant dish features cauliflower prepared two ways: in steak form, it's visually pretty, and you don't waste anything, as the leftovers are used to prepare a creamy purée. It's all served with a fresh dip.

1. **TO MAKE THE CAULIFLOWER STEAKS:** Preheat the oven to 390°F (200°C) on the convection setting. Line a baking sheet with parchment paper. Cut 2 large slices, about 1 inch (2.5 cm) thick, from the center of the cauliflower. Detach the remaining florets and reserve them for the puree. Place the steaks on the prepared baking sheet.

2. In a small bowl, mix the 3 tablespoons oil, smoked paprika, paprika, garlic powder, and salt and pepper to taste until well combined. Brush both sides of the cauliflower steaks with this mixture. Roast for 25 to 30 minutes, flipping halfway through, until the slices are golden brown and tender.

3. **MEANWHILE, MAKE THE CAULIFLOWER PURÉE:** Bring a large pot of water to a boil. Once boiling, add the reserved cauliflower florets and garlic clove and cook for 15 to 20 minutes, until tender. Drain well and transfer to a blender. Add the crème fraiche, butter, and salt to taste to the blender and blend until smooth. (If needed, add a little water or milk to adjust the consistency of the purée.)

4. **TO MAKE THE OLIVE, LEMON, AND PARSLEY DIP:** In a medium bowl, mix all the dip ingredients until well combined.

5. Divide the cauliflower purée between two plates, then place a cauliflower steak on top and drizzle with a spoonful of the olive, lemon, and parsley dip. Finish with some black pepper and garnish with a few olives.

SIDES

Olive Oil and Lemon Mashed Potatoes

PURÉE DE POMMES DE TERRE
À L'HUILE D'OLIVE ET AU CITRON

This is a light and refreshing mashed-potato recipe with no milk, cream, or butter—only potatoes, olive oil, garlic, thyme, and lemon. The result is a smooth mash with a lovely lemon note.

YIELD 4 SERVINGS
PREP TIME 10 MINUTES
COOK TIME 30 MINUTES

2¼ pounds (1 kg) starchy potatoes (such as russet or Yukon Gold), peeled and cut into large pieces

2 teaspoons coarse salt

2 cloves garlic, peeled

10 sprigs fresh thyme

1 medium lemon, for peeling and juicing

½ cup (120 ml) olive oil

Fleur de sel or sea salt flakes

1 Place the potatoes in a large pot of cold water and bring to a boil. As soon as it starts to bubble, add the coarse salt and garlic cloves, reduce the heat to medium, and cook the potatoes for 25 to 30 minutes, until fork-tender. Drain, reserving ½ cup (120 ml) of the cooking water.

2 Meanwhile, remove the leaves from the thyme sprigs. Use a peeler to remove 3 large pieces of peel from the lemon, then slice the lemon in half and squeeze 2 tablespoons of juice into a cup or small bowl to use later.

3 In a small saucepan, heat the oil with the lemon peels and thyme leaves over low heat for 5 minutes. Remove from the heat and let the oil infuse while the potatoes are cooking.

4 Mash the potatoes and garlic cloves using a potato masher. Pour in the infused oil, reserved lemon juice and reserved cooking water and mix well. Add a generous pinch of fleur de sel. Serve warm (see Note).

———

note These mashed potatoes go well with the recipes for Herbed Bacon-Wrapped Pork Tenderloin (page 87) and Cod Loins with Pistachio Crust (page 107).

Roasted Fennel and Arugula Pesto

FENOUIL RÔTI
ET PESTO DE ROQUETTE

This is one of my favorite ways to serve fennel! The combination of arugula pesto and fresh fennel is just perfect. I like to serve it as a side dish or an appetizer.

1 **TO MAKE THE ROASTED FENNEL:** Preheat the oven to 390°F (200°C) on the convection setting. Line a baking sheet with parchment paper.

2 Remove the hard ends of the fennel bulbs and the fronds (you can reserve the fronds for garnishing). Place the fennel bulb vertically on its base and cut 5 or 6 thin slices lengthwise and place the slices on the prepared baking sheet.

3 Brush both sides of the slices with the 2 tablespoons oil and season with salt and pepper. Roast in the oven for 25 to 30 minutes, until tender.

4 **MEANWHILE, MAKE THE ARUGULA PESTO:** Place all the pesto ingredients into a blender and blend until smooth.

5 Arrange the roasted fennel on a serving platter topped with the arugula pesto and fennel fronds (if using). Serve the remaining arugula pesto on the side (see Notes).

———

notes You can vary this recipe with any oven-roasted vegetables, such as baby potatoes, zucchini, carrots, or squash.

Serve this roasted fennel with the Herbed Bacon-Wrapped Pork Tenderloin (page 87) or the Tomato Tarte Tatin (page 125).

YIELD 4 SERVINGS
PREP TIME 10 MINUTES
COOK TIME 30 MINUTES

ROASTED FENNEL

4 large fennel bulbs (see Notes)

2 tablespoons olive oil

Salt and black pepper

ARUGULA PESTO

3 cups (60 g) arugula

½ cup (60 g) whole roasted hazelnuts

½ cup (60 g) grated Parmesan cheese

2 garlic cloves, peeled

½ cup (120 ml) olive oil

3 tablespoons fresh lemon juice

1 pinch fleur de sel or sea salt

Healthy Oven-Baked French Fries

FRITES SAINES AU FOUR

French fries are certainly the most classic of all French bistro side dishes, but did you know you could make a healthier version at home, in the oven and with just a few tablespoons of olive oil? The result is amazing: crispy french fries that taste just as good as if they were deep-fried.

YIELD 2 OR 3 SERVINGS
PREP TIME 5 MINUTES, PLUS 30 MINUTES SOAKING
COOK TIME 30 MINUTES

2¼ pounds (1 kg) starchy potatoes, peeled or skins on

3 tablespoons sunflower or olive oil

Salt

Homemade Mayonnaise (page 12), for serving (optional)

Ketchup, for serving (optional)

1 Preheat the oven to 420°F (210°C) on the convection setting. Line a baking sheet with parchment paper.

2 Wash the potatoes and cut them into fries. Rinse the fries under cold water, then place them in a large bowl. Cover with cold water and let soak for 30 minutes. Drain the fries and dry them well with a clean towel, making sure they are as dry as possible. Lightly rinse and dry the bowl, then place the potatoes back into it.

3 Add the oil and the salt to taste and mix gently with your hands to coat the fries. Immediately spread the fries on the prepared baking sheet in a single layer, making sure they are not overlapping, and place in the oven (they will release water if they sit too long before baking and not turn out crispy).

4 Bake for 30 to 35 minutes, turning them every 10 minutes, until golden and crispy. (You can also bake them in an air fryer for 20 to 25 minutes at 390°F (200°C), shaking them after 10 minutes.)

5 Serve immediately with mayonnaise (if using) and/or ketchup (if using) (see Note).

───────

note These fries can be served for almost any occasion and go particularly well with the Steak with Garlic, Lemon, and Herb Butter (page 101) and the Salmon Tartare with Dill and Pink Peppercorns (page 104).

Green Beans with Crunchy Honey Almonds

HARICOTS
AUX AMANDES CROQUANTES AU MIEL

This is an upgraded version of the classic French green beans with almonds in which I bake the almonds with honey to make them crunchy. Doing this adds just a hint of crispiness and caramelization to the beans without being overly sweet, making it a delightful side dish.

1 **TO MAKE THE CRUNCHY HONEY ALMONDS:** Preheat the oven to 325°F (160°C) on the convection setting. Line a baking sheet with parchment paper,

2 Stir together the honey, water, and pinch of salt in a small saucepan and heat over low heat until the honey is liquid. Remove from the heat and gently mix in the sliced almonds. Spread the almonds on the prepared baking sheet.

3 Bake for 15 to 18 minutes, until golden. Let cool, then break apart if needed.

4 **MEANWHILE, MAKE THE GREEN BEANS:** Bring a large pot of salted water to a boil. Meanwhile, prepare a large bowl with cold water and ice for an ice bath. Add the green beans and cook for 7 to 10 minutes, until slightly tender. Drain, then transfer the beans to the ice bath for 3 minutes. Drain again.

5 In a large skillet, melt the butter over medium heat. Add the shallot and garlic and sauté until both start to brown. Add the green beans and sauté for 5 minutes, or until the beans are slightly softened. Season with salt and pepper.

6 Right before serving, sprinkle some crunchy honey almonds over the beans and toss gently.

———

note Pair as a side dish with the Tuna Steak with Tomato, Olives, and Capers (page 117) or the Creamy Tarragon and Mushroom Chicken (page 98).

YIELD 4 SERVINGS
PREP TIME 10 MINUTES
COOK TIME 20 MINUTES

CRUNCHY HONEY ALMONDS

2 tablespoons honey
(adjust if needed)

1 tablespoon water

1 pinch salt

⅔ cup (60 g) sliced unsalted almonds

GREEN BEANS

Salt

1 pound (455 g) fresh green beans, stems trimmed

2 tablespoons unsalted butter

1 medium shallot, finely chopped

2 cloves garlic, minced

Black pepper

Rustic Gratin Dauphinois

GRATIN DAUPHINOIS RUSTIQUE

This rustic and quick version of gratin dauphinois brings a touch of comfort to your meals. Traditionally, we don't add cheese to this dish, but I like to sprinkle some between the potato layers to get a cheesy texture.

YIELD 4 SERVINGS
PREP TIME 15 MINUTES, PLUS 30 MINUTES RESTING
COOK TIME 1 HOUR 5 MINUTES

¾ cup (180 ml) heavy whipping cream

1¼ cups (300 ml) whole milk

4 sprigs fresh thyme

2 bay leaves

2 cloves garlic, minced

¼ teaspoon ground nutmeg

Salt and black pepper

2¼ pounds (1 kg) starchy potatoes (such as russet or Yukon Gold), peeled or skins on

1 tablespoon unsalted butter

1 cup (100 g) grated Swiss cheese (such as Emmental or Gruyère)

1 Preheat the oven to 390 °F (200°C) on the convection setting.

2 In a medium saucepan, combine the cream, milk, thyme, bay leaves, and garlic over medium-low heat and cook for 5 minutes, stirring occasionally. Add the nutmeg and season with salt and pepper. Remove from the heat and let sit for 30 minutes so that the flavors infuse.

3 Meanwhile, thinly slice the potatoes with a mandoline (see Notes). Place them in a medium bowl, season with salt and pepper, and toss well. Grease a gratin dish with the butter. Arrange one-third of the potato slices in the dish, then sprinkle with half of the cheese. Layer another third of the potato slices, then sprinkle with the remaining cheese. Top with the remaining potato slices.

4 Remove the thyme sprigs and bay leaves from the infused cream and discard. Gently pour the cream-milk mixture over the potatoes. Bake for 1 hour, or until the potatoes are tender and turning golden brown. If the potatoes start to blacken, cover them with aluminum foil or parchment paper. Turn off the oven, open the door, and let the gratin stand in the oven for 15 more minutes to finish cooking and allow the potatoes to absorb the liquid. Serve warm (see Notes).

―――――

notes Don't wash the potatoes after slicing them to preserve their starch, which acts as a natural binder for the gratin.

Pair as a side dish with the Herbed Bacon-Wrapped Pork Tenderloin (page 87) or serve as a main with a salad.

Rice Pilaf with Caramelized Shallots, Dried Apricots, and Cashews

RIZ PILAF
AUX ÉCHALOTES CARAMÉLISÉES, ABRICOTS SECS ET NOIX DE CAJOU

Rice pilaf is originally from the Middle East and, over time, has become popular in French cuisine, particularly as an accompaniment to poultry dishes. In this fusion version, I've added a French touch through dried apricots and caramelized shallots, with some roasted cashews for crunch.

1 **TO MAKE THE ROASTED CASHEWS:** Preheat the oven to 350°F (175°C) on the convection setting. Line a baking sheet with parchment paper.

2 In a small bowl, mix the cashews with the 1 tablespoon oil, pinch of salt, smoked paprika and garlic powder until well coated. Spread the cashews on the prepared baking sheet. Roast for 15 to 20 minutes, until golden and crispy.

3 **MEANWHILE, MAKE THE RICE PILAF:** In a medium saucepan, heat the 2 tablespoons oil over medium-high heat. Add the shallots and sauté for 5 to 10 minutes, stirring regularly, until they are well caramelized. Remove from the pan.

4 In the same saucepan, melt the butter over medium heat. Once melted, add the rice and cook, stirring, for 2 minutes. Add the broth and bay leaf, then bring to a boil. Once boiling, reduce the heat to low, cover with the lid, and let simmer for 18 to 20 minutes, until the liquid is absorbed. Remove the pan from the heat, fluff the rice with a fork, and let rest for 5 minutes.

5 In a serving bowl, combine the cooked rice, caramelized shallots, chopped cilantro, dried apricots, and roasted cashews and mix well. Season with salt and pepper. Serve warm or lukewarm (see Note).

note Serve this pilaf as a side dish with grilled meats or enjoy it lukewarm as a main course paired with a salad or the Chilled Zucchini and Pea Soup (page 44).

YIELD 4 SERVINGS
PREP TIME 10 MINUTES
COOK TIME 30 MINUTES

ROASTED CASHEWS

⅓ cup (40 g) whole cashews

1 tablespoon olive oil

1 pinch salt

½ teaspoon smoked paprika

½ teaspoon garlic powder

RICE PILAF

2 tablespoons olive oil

2 shallots, sliced into thin rounds

1 tablespoon unsalted butter

1 cup (200 g) long-grain white rice

1¾ cups (420 ml) chicken broth

1 bay leaf

⅓ cup (15 g) finely chopped fresh cilantro

⅓ cup (85 g) chopped dried apricots

Salt and black pepper

RATATOUILLE
DE LÉGUMES CONFITS AU FOUR

Ratatouille is traditionally a dish in which each vegetable is sautéed separately in a pot before being combined. Personally, I prefer this oven version; the vegetables cook all together for a long time at a low temperature, resulting in super-juicy, confit vegetables. And it's much quicker to prepare!

YIELD 4 SERVINGS
PREP TIME 10 MINUTES
COOK TIME 2 HOURS

2 medium zucchini, cut into
1-inch (2.5 cm) cubes

1 large eggplant,
cut into 1-inch (2.5 cm) cubes

1 medium yellow bell pepper,
cut into 1-inch (2.5 cm) cubes

1 medium green bell pepper,
cut into 1-inch (2.5 cm) cubes

5 medium tomatoes,
cut into 6 wedges

5 cloves garlic,
smashed and chopped

Salt and black pepper

⅓ cup (80 ml) olive oil

1 tablespoon balsamic vinegar

6 sprigs fresh thyme or
2 tablespoons dried thyme

1 Preheat the oven to 350°F (180°C) on the convection setting.

2 Place the zucchini, eggplant, yellow and green bell peppers, tomatoes, and garlic in an oven-safe dish, about 9 x 11 inches (24 x 30 cm; the dish shouldn't be too big so that the juices don't dry out). Season generously with salt and pepper, drizzle with the oil and balsamic vinegar, and add the thyme. Mix well.

3 Cover the vegetables with a sheet of parchment paper or aluminum foil to prevent them from getting dark and allow the vegetables to release their juices.

4 Bake for 30 minutes. Remove the parchment paper or aluminum foil, stir carefully, and continue baking for another 1 hour and 30 minutes, stirring every 15 to 30 minutes (this is very important) to prevent the vegetables from drying out. The vegetables are ready when they are juicy and tender. Serve warm (see Note).

———

note This ratatouille can be enjoyed with the Marinated Pork Chops with Herbes de Provence (page 94), the Baked Salmon with Almond, Green Olive, and Preserved Lemon Salsa (page 113), and the Sunday Roast Lemon Chicken with Vegetables (page 84), or eat it cold on crusty bread.

DESSERTS

Raspberry and Almond Clafoutis

CLAFOUTIS
AUX FRAMBOISES ET AUX AMANDES

This is a butter-free dessert, except for greasing the dish, that has a custard-like texture. Traditionally made with cherries, it can be made with any seasonal fruit. I really like this version with raspberries and a little ground almond in the batter.

YIELD 6 SERVINGS
PREP TIME 10 MINUTES
COOK TIME 35 MINUTES

1 tablespoon unsalted butter

½ cup (100 g) caster sugar, plus 1 tablespoon for the tart pan

3 medium eggs

1 pinch salt

½ cup (50 g) ground almonds

⅔ cup (80 g) all-purpose flour

1¼ cups (300 ml) whole or almond milk

1 teaspoon vanilla extract

2 cups fresh (250 g) or frozen (280 g) raspberries

Confectioners' sugar, for dusting (optional)

1   Preheat the oven to 350°F (180°C) on the convection setting. Grease a 9-inch (23 cm) tart pan with the butter and sprinkle it with the 1 tablespoon caster sugar; this will allow the clafoutis to develop a caramelized crust.

2   In a large bowl, beat the eggs with the ½ cup (100 g) caster sugar and salt until well combined (see Note).

3   Gradually add the ground almonds and flour while whisking continuously to avoid lumps. Slowly whisk in the milk and finish with the vanilla.

4   Pour the batter into the prepared pan and spread the raspberries evenly on top.

5   Bake for 30 to 35 minutes, until the edges are done and the center is still slightly runny. It will set as it cools. Let cool slightly before serving. Dust with confectioners' sugar (if using).

6   Slice and serve it as individual portions or present it family-style by placing it in the center of the table and providing spoons for everyone to help themselves.

———

note   It is important to mix the batter by hand with a whisk or fork to avoid creating air bubbles. The batter for clafoutis is similar to a crêpe batter in that it is runnier.

Chocolate Fondants

MOELLEUX AU CHOCOLAT

This is my absolute-favorite dessert and a classic for all chocolate fans.

1 Preheat the oven to 350°F (180°C) on the convection setting. Grease six to eight 3½-inch (9 cm) ramekins with butter. Cut 6 to 8 circles of parchment paper that are the same diameter as the ramekins.

2 Melt the 1⅓ cups (220 g) dark chocolate and butter in a double boiler or small saucepan over low heat. Remove from the heat and let cool slightly.

3 In a large bowl, whisk together the eggs and caster sugar until light and fluffy. Add the flour and stir in the melted chocolate until everything is well combined.

4 Add a circle of parchment paper to the bottom of each ramekin to make it easier to remove the fondants. Fill each ramekin two-thirds full with the batter. Press down a chocolate square in the center of each ramekin. Bake for 12 to 14 minutes, until desired texture (for a melting heart, follow the shorter baking time; for a creamy texture, follow the longer time). Let cool for 5 minutes; the center should set a little, yet be runny and velvety.

5 Serve warm either in the ramekins or place a plate on top of each ramekin and carefully turn it over to plate it. Dust with confectioners' sugar (if using) and serve with vanilla ice cream or crème anglaise.

notes You can use 2½-inch (6.5 cm) muffin pans to make 12 to 14 fondants, but only bake them for 7 to 9 minutes

The batter can be made up to 24 hours in advance and refrigerated.

YIELD 6 TO 8 FONDANTS (SEE NOTES)
PREP TIME 10 MINUTES
COOK TIME 12 MINUTES

1⅓ cups (220 g) dark chocolate (50% cacao), plus 1 square of dark chocolate per cake

⅔ cup (160 g) unsalted butter, plus more for greasing

4 medium eggs

⅔ cup (135 g) caster sugar

½ cup (60 g) all-purpose flour

1 tablespoon confectioners' sugar, for dusting (optional)

Vanilla ice cream or Crème Anglaise (page 183), for serving

Apricot, Almond, and Pistachio Tart

TARTE AUX ABRICOTS
AMANDES ET PISTACHES

If there's one fruit I absolutely adore, it's the apricot! An apricot and almond tart is already one of my favorite desserts, but by adding pistachio cream and crushed pistachios, this tart becomes fabulous.

YIELD 8 SERVINGS
PREP TIME 20 MINUTES, PLUS 1 HOUR CHILLING
COOK TIME 40 MINUTES

1 medium egg

⅓ cup (65 g) brown sugar

¼ cup (60 g) unsalted butter, at room temperature, plus more for greasing

⅔ cup (65 g) ground almonds

2 tablespoons (30 g) pistachio paste

½ teaspoon vanilla extract

1 chilled ball Sweet Shortcrust Pastry (pâte brisée sucrée; page 14)

All-purpose flour, for dusting

1⅓ pounds (600 g) apricots, cut into quarters

⅓ cup (25 g) chopped unsalted pistachios

1   In a small bowl, whisk together the egg and sugar until the mixture turns pale. Stir in the softened butter, ground almonds, pistachio paste, and vanilla and mix until it is a smooth cream.

2   Preheat the oven to 350°F (180°C) on the convection setting. Line the bottom of an 11-inch (28 cm) tart pan with a circle of parchment paper cut to the pan's diameter. Lightly grease the pan's edges with butter.

3   Take the chilled dough out of the refrigerator, place it on a floured surface, and let it warm up for 5 minutes. Roll out the dough with a rolling pin into a circle at least 2 inches (5 cm) larger in diameter than the tart pan. Transfer the dough to the prepared pan. Trim off any excess dough from the edges. Prick the base of the dough with a fork. Lay a sheet of parchment paper over the dough and fill it with pie weights, dried beans, or uncooked rice. Blind-bake it for 10 to 15 minutes, or until the edges start to harden. Remove from the oven, leaving the oven on.

4   Pour the pistachio cream into the prebaked crust. (The cream will rise during baking, so it's okay if it seems like too little.) Arrange the apricot quarters on top of the cream and sprinkle with the chopped pistachios. Bake for 25 to 30 minutes, until the filling is set and the crust is golden brown. If the apricots start to blacken while baking, cover with aluminum foil or parchment paper. Let cool to room temperature, then refrigerate for 1 hour before slicing and serving to ensure the pistachio cream is well set.

Orange and Cardamom Crème Brûlée

CRÈME BRÛLÉE
À L'ORANGE ET À LA CARDAMOM

This is an elegant twist on the classic crème brûlée. The combination of vanilla, cardamom, and orange zest is a true delight.

1   In a small saucepan, combine the milk, cream, vanilla, and cardamom. Heat over medium heat until it starts to simmer. Remove from heat, then grate in the orange zest. Let sit for at least 30 minutes to infuse the flavors.

2   Preheat the oven to 250°F (120°C) on the convection setting. Bring a kettle or pot of water to a boil.

3   In a large bowl, whisk together the egg yolks and caster sugar until the mixture turns pale. Add the milk-cream mixture and mix well. Remove any pale foam from the top of the liquid.

4   Pour the mixture into six 4-inch (10 cm) ramekins that are 1 inch (2.5 cm) tall, filling each one three-quarters full. Place the ramekins on a baking tray or in a roasting pan and pour boiling water around them to cover three-quarters of the ramekins and to create a water bath (bain-marie). Bake for 40 to 50 minutes, until the cream is set; shake the ramekins: if the cream slightly jiggles in the center but not at the edges, they are done. Refrigerate for at least 4 hours.

5   Right before serving, sprinkle brown sugar over the tops and caramelize the crèmes brûlées with a culinary torch or under the oven broiler for a few minutes.

note You can prepare these crèmes brûlées a day or two in advance, but don't caramelize the sugar topping until right before serving; otherwise, it will lose its crunch.

YIELD 6 CRÈMES BRÛLÉES
PREP TIME 10 MINUTES, PLUS 4 HOURS 30 MINUTES RESTING AND CHILLING
COOK TIME 50 MINUTES

1 cup (240 ml) whole milk

1 cup (240 ml) heavy whipping cream

¼ teaspoon vanilla powder or 1 teaspoon vanilla extract

¼ teaspoon ground cardamom

1 large orange, for zesting

5 medium egg yolks

¼ cup (50 g) caster sugar

¼ cup (50 g) brown or caster sugar

Mini Lemon Meringue Tarts

TARTELETTES
AU CITRON MERINGUÉES

These mini lemon meringue tarts are a classic of French bakeries. It's a perfect treat for lemon lovers!

YIELD 6 MINI TARTS
PREP TIME 15 MINUTES,
PLUS 2 HOURS 10 MINUTES
CHILLING
COOK TIME 30 MINUTES

SWEET SHORTCRUST PASTRY
Unsalted butter, for greasing

1 chilled ball Sweet Shortcrust
Pastry (pâte sablée; page 15)

All-purpose flour, for dusting

LEMON CURD
3 medium eggs

⅔ cup (130 g) caster sugar

2 medium lemons, for zesting
and juicing

3 tablespoons cornstarch

¼ cup (60 g) unsalted butter,
at room temperature

MERINGUE
2 medium egg whites

⅓ cup (65 g) caster sugar

1 Preheat the oven to 320°F (160°C) on the convection setting. Grease six 4-inch (10 cm) mini tart pans with butter

2 **TO PREPARE THE SWEET SHORTCRUST PASTRY:** Place the chilled dough ball on a lightly floured surface and divide it into 6 equal-size pieces. Roll out each piece into a circle slightly thicker than ⅛ inch (3 mm) and transfer to a prepared tart pan. Trim off any excess dough and prick the base with a fork. Lay a piece of parchment paper over the dough and fill it with pie weights, dried beans, or uncooked rice. Bake for 20 to 25 minutes, until the crust is golden brown and cooked through. Transfer to a wire rack and let cool for 10 minutes, then carefully remove the crusts from the pans.

3 **TO MAKE THE LEMON CURD:** In a medium bowl, whisk together the eggs and ⅔ cup (130 g) caster sugar until the mixture turns pale. In a medium saucepan, mix grated lemon zest from 1 lemon, ½ cup (120 ml) lemon juice (squeezed from both lemons), and cornstarch until the cornstarch is dissolved. Pour the egg-sugar mixture into the saucepan and cook over medium-low heat, stirring continuously, until the curd thickens. Remove the pan from the heat, add the ¼ cup (60 g) butter, and stir until incorporated. Immediately spread the curd over the cooled crusts. Let set in the refrigerator for at least 2 hours.

4 **TO MAKE THE MERINGUE:** In a large bowl, beat the egg whites with a hand mixer, gradually adding the ⅓ cup (65 g) caster sugar when they begin to stiffen. Continue beating until firm peaks form and the sugar is dissolved. Spoon the meringue over the curd. Use a culinary torch to lightly brown it; alternatively, bake the tarts in a 390°F (200°C) oven for 5 to 10 minutes, until the meringue begins to color. Serve immediately, or chilled for up to 48 hours.

Vanilla Poached Pears with Crème Anglaise

POIRES POCHÉES
À LA VANILLE ET CRÈME ANGLAISE

These poached pears are a simple, elegant dessert. The velvety crème anglaise, also known as vanilla custard sauce, deliciously highlights this fruit. In the summer, try this recipe with peaches.

1 **TO MAKE THE CRÈME ANGLAISE:** In a medium saucepan, bring the milk, cream, and vanilla extract to a boil over medium heat. Remove the pan from the heat and let the mixture cool to 175°F (80°C). In a medium bowl, whisk the egg yolks with the ⅓ cup (65 g) sugar until doubled in volume. Gradually stir in 2 ladlefuls of the milk-cream mixture to temper the eggs. Pour the entire egg-cream mixture into the saucepan and heat over low heat, stirring continuously. The custard will thicken at 175 to 180°F (around 80°C). Do not exceed this temperature, as the eggs may coagulate. Once thickened, remove from the heat, cover with plastic wrap to prevent a skin from forming, and let cool to room temperature. Refrigerate until ready to serve.

2 **TO MAKE THE POACHED PEARS:** Peel the pears, keeping the stems, and cut them in half lengthwise. Remove the cores. In a medium saucepan, combine the ½ cup (100 g) sugar, cinnamon stick, and star anise with 4 cups (960 ml) of water. Scrape out the seeds from the split vanilla bean with the tip of a knife and add to the saucepan, along with the pod halves. Bring the mixture to a boil over high heat, then reduce the heat to medium-low. Add the pear halves and let simmer for 15 to 20 minutes, until the tip of a knife or a toothpick can be inserted and removed smoothly. Remove the pears from the pan.

3 To serve, pour some crème anglaise into shallow bowls, then add 2 warm poached pear halves on top.

YIELD 6 SERVINGS
PREP TIME 10 MINUTES
COOK TIME 30 MINUTES

CRÈME ANGLAISE

1 cup (240 ml) whole milk

1 cup (240 ml) heavy whipping cream

1 teaspoon vanilla extract

5 medium egg yolks

⅓ cup (65 g) granulated sugar

POACHED PEARS

6 pears, preferably a ripe but firm variety (such as Conference, Anjou, Bosc, or Bartlett)

½ cup (100 g) granulated sugar

1 cinnamon stick

2 star anise

1 vanilla bean, split in half lengthwise

SABLÉS À LA LAVANDE
ET SALADE DE FRAISES

These lavender cookies and strawberry salad are the perfect summer match. I love how the cookies' delicate hint of lavender pairs perfectly with their buttery crispness, while the fresh strawberry salad adds a burst of fruity sweetness. This combination is my go-to for a light, elegant finish to any meal, bringing a touch of sophistication without any fuss.

YIELD 24 COOKIES AND
6 SALAD SERVINGS
PREP TIME 10 MINUTES,
PLUS 30 MINUTES CHILLING
COOK TIME 12 MINUTES

LAVENDER SHORTBREAD COOKIES

1⅔ cups (200 g)
all-purpose flour

½ cup (50 g) ground almonds

1 tablespoon plus
1 teaspoon dried lavender

½ cup (100 g) caster sugar

1 pinch salt

⅔ cup (160 g) unsalted butter,
at room temperature

1 medium egg yolk

STRAWBERRY SALAD

1 pound (455 g) strawberries,
hulled and cut in half

2 tablespoons fresh lemon juice

3 tablespoons
brown sugar

1 **TO MAKE THE LAVENDER SHORTBREAD COOKIES:** In a large bowl, combine the flour, ground almonds, lavender, caster sugar, and salt. Add the butter and mix until a sandy texture forms.

2 Add the egg yolk and continue mixing until a homogeneous dough forms. Shape the dough into a log 12 inches (30 cm) long and 1½ inches (4 cm) in diameter. Wrap it in plastic wrap and refrigerate for at least 30 minutes, or overnight.

3 Preheat the oven to 350°F (180 °C) on the convection setting. Line a baking sheet with parchment paper.

4 Using a sharp knife, slice the chilled dough log into ½-inch-thick (1.5 cm) rounds. Place the cookies on the prepared baking sheet, leaving at least 1 inch (2.5 cm) between each cookie. Bake for 12 to 15 minutes, until the edges just start to color. Transfer to wire rack and let cool (see Note).

5 **MEANWHILE, MAKE THE STRAWBERRY SALAD:** Place the strawberries, lemon juice, and brown sugar in a small bowl and mix well. Let sit for 15 minutes to infuse the flavors.

6 Divide the strawberry salad among bowls and serve with the lavender shortbread cookies.

———

note Once the cookies have cooled, store them in an airtight container at room temperature for up to 1 week.

Roasted Peaches with Yogurt Ice Cream and Toasted Buckwheat

PÊCHES RÔTIES

AVEC GLACE AU YAOURT ET SARRASIN GRILLÉ

In summer, this is the perfect dessert to end a meal on a light, sweet note. The peaches, roasted with butter, almost melt in your mouth, and the yogurt ice cream is very refreshing. The toasted buckwheat adds a nice nutty flavor. You can also make this recipe with apricots or plums.

1   **TO MAKE THE TOASTED BUCKWHEAT:** Place the buckwheat in a dry medium skillet (without any oil) and toast over medium heat for a couple of minutes, or until it turns golden brown. Remove from the pan.

2   **TO MAKE THE ROASTED PEACHES:** Preheat the oven to 350°F (180°C) on the convection setting. Grease an oven-safe dish with butter; the dish should be just large enough to hold the peach halves without them overlapping too much, ensuring they fit snugly. Place the peaches in the prepared dish, cut sides up.

3   In a medium bowl, mix the melted butter, cinnamon, brown sugar, and 1 teaspoon vanilla. Brush the mixture over the peach halves, ensuring they are well coated and allowing it to drizzle down their sides. Bake, uncovered, for about 30 minutes, or until the peaches are fork-tender.

4   **TO MAKE THE YOGURT ICE CREAM:** In a large bowl, mix all the ice cream ingredients until well combined, then chill in the refrigerator for 1 hour. Pour the chilled mixture into an ice cream maker and churn until the ice cream has a soft-serve texture. If you don't have an ice cream maker, place the mixture in a metal cake pan, cover with plastic wrap, and freeze for 2 hours, stirring with a spoon every 30 minutes, or until the ice cream reaches the desired consistency.

5   Serve a warm roasted peach half with a big scoop or 2 small scoops of yogurt ice cream in bowls and top with toasted buckwheat for crunch.

YIELD 4 SERVINGS
PREP TIME 10 MINUTES, PLUS 1 HOUR CHILLING
COOK TIME 30 MINUTES

TOASTED BUCKWHEAT

¼ cup (50 g) buckwheat groats

ROASTED PEACHES

2 tablespoons unsalted butter, melted, plus more for greasing

2 peaches, cut in half

1 pinch cinnamon

1 tablespoon brown sugar

1 teaspoon vanilla extract

YOGURT ICE CREAM

2 cups (480 g) plain yogurt

1 cup crème fraiche (240 g) or heavy whipping cream (240 ml)

⅔ cup (85 g) confectioners' sugar, sifted

Vanilla extract

MOUSSE AU CHOCOLAT
À LA CHANTILLY AUX ÉPICES DE NOËL

Here's a dessert that combines two of my favorite French treats: mousse au chocolat and crème Chantilly. I have added some spices to the whipped cream to give this dessert a subtle festive note.

YIELD 6 TO 8 SERVINGS
PREP TIME 20 MINUTES, PLUS 2 HOURS CHILLING

CHOCOLATE MOUSSE

6 medium eggs, at room temperature, yolks and whites separated, divided

7 ounces (200 g) dark chocolate (50 to 60% cacao)

2 teaspoons vanilla extract

1 pinch fleur de sel or sea salt flakes

CHANTILLY CREAM

1 cup (240 ml) cold crème fleurette or heavy whipping cream

1 vanilla bean, split in half lengthwise, or 2 teaspoons vanilla extract

⅓ cup (30 g) confectioners' sugar

¼ teaspoon ground cinnamon

1 pinch ground nutmeg

1 pinch ground cloves

1 **TO MAKE THE CHOCOLATE MOUSSE:** Melt the chocolate in a bain-marie by placing it in a heatproof bowl over a pot of simmering water. Stir until the chocolate is completely smooth, then let cool slightly to keep it liquid and not cook the eggs. In a large bowl, mix the egg yolks, vanilla extract, and fleur de sel. Gradually fold in the melted chocolate with a spatula, mixing well.

2 In another large bowl, beat the egg whites with a hand mixer until stiff peaks form. Gently fold the egg whites into the chocolate mixture in 3 or 4 additions, taking care not to deflate it. Pour the mousse into six to eight 3-inch (7.5 cm) ramekins, cover with plastic wrap, and refrigerate for at least 2 hours, or preferably 4 and up to 48 hours.

3 **TO MAKE THE CHANTILLY CREAM:** Five minutes before making the Chantilly cream, place the crème fleurette and a medium mixing bowl, if possible, in the freezer. If using the vanilla bean, scrape out the seeds with the tip of a knife. In a small bowl, mix together the confectioners' sugar, vanilla, cinnamon, nutmeg, and cloves, then sift to obtain a fine powder. Add the cold crème to the chilled bowl and whip with a hand mixer or electric whisk until it begins to thicken. Add the sugar-spice mixture and continue whisking until stiff peaks form.

4 Right before serving, remove the mousse from the refrigerator and pipe the whipped cream on top or add a dollop with a spoon. Serve immediately.

Classic Apple Tarte Tatin

TARTE TATIN
AUX POMMES CLASSIQUE

This is the most iconic French dessert and one of my absolute favorites. I never miss a chance to order it when I spot it on a menu. This recipe is made with a classic shortcrust pastry and rich butter caramel. If you've never tried making it before, trust me, it's much easier than you might think.

1   Right before making the caramel, peel and core the apples, then cut them into quarters.

2   In a large skillet, evenly distribute the sugar. Let the sugar melt over medium heat for 6 to 8 minutes, until completely melted and golden. (It's very important not to touch the sugar; otherwise, it might crystallize.) Reduce the heat to medium-low and add the butter, stirring vigorously for 3 to 4 minutes, until the mixture is smooth. If the sugar begins to darken too much, remove the pan from the heat. Add the apple quarters to the pan and mix well to coat the apples with the caramel. Scrape out the seeds from the split vanilla bean with the tip of a knife and add to the apples. (You can also add the pod halves for extra flavor and remove before baking.) Cook over low heat for 15 to 20 minutes, stirring regularly, until the apples start to become tender.

3   Preheat the oven to 350°F (180°C). Arrange the apple quarters in the bottom of a 9-inch (23 cm) tart or cake pan, positioning them vertically and tightly in a circle . Pour the caramel over the apples.

4   Place the chilled dough on a lightly floured surface and roll it out with a rolling pin into a circle slightly larger than the tart pan. Place the pastry circle over the apples, tucking the edges inside the pan. Bake for 40 to 45 minutes, until the pastry is golden and firm. Let cool for 10 minutes to allow the caramel to set. Run the tip of a knife around the crust to detach it from the pan. Place a serving plate on top of the pan and carefully flip it over in one movement. Slice and serve warm.

YIELD 8 SERVINGS
PREP TIME 15 MINUTES
COOK TIME 1 HOUR

8 small, firm, and juicy apples (such as Golden Delicious or Granny Smith)

½ cup (100 g) granulated sugar

¼ cup (60 g) unsalted butter, cut into small cubes

1 vanilla bean, split in half lengthwise

1 chilled ball Classic Shortcrust Pastry (page 13; or substitute with a thawed store-bought, high-quality puff pastry made with butter)

All-purpose flour, for dusting

ACKNOWLEDGMENTS

I would like to express my deepest gratitude to everyone who played a part in the creation of this cookbook.

To my parents, who not only instilled in me a love of French cuisine from an early age, but who also shaped me into the person I am today. You taught me to be independent, strong, and to believe in my projects. Without your guidance and support, none of this would have been possible.

A heartfelt thank you to Alexander Arfert, my partner, for your daily love and patience. You were my first tester, tasting every dish with care and helping me perfect the recipes. You also comforted me in times of doubt and always believed in me.

A huge thanks to Mechthild Arfert, for your invaluable help in the kitchen and during the photoshoots, and for your advice that elevated every dish presented in this book.

I am also very grateful to all my friends and family, who were always incredibly supportive. I feel so lucky to be surrounded by people who share my love for food and the joy of coming together over a good meal.

I would like to thank Claire von Vaernewyck, for stepping in at the last minute during the recipe-testing phase. Your support made it possible to ensure that every recipe in this book is tested and foolproof.

Finally, an enormous merci to my incredible community, whose daily positive comments and energy fuel my passion and give me the strength to pursue my dreams. This book exists because of your unwavering support. I am deeply grateful for each and every one of you who has stood by me throughout this journey.

I want to extend my heartfelt gratitude to my entire community, with a special thank-you to the dedicated recipe testers who made this book possible. Every recipe in these pages has been meticulously tested multiple times by a diverse group of testers from around the globe. This extensive testing was essential to ensure that each recipe would be reliable, no matter where you are located and regardless of your oven or level of expertise. Thanks to their invaluable feedback, with each of them testing two or three recipes, I was able to refine and perfect the recipes to offer you the best possible results.

Merci à . . .

Addie Brobbey, Addie O'Beirne, Adele Chong Wedekind, Adriana Pop, Agate Daiga Ozoliņa , Agathe Paul, Agnès M., Agnieszka Białas, Agnieszka Sobolak, Alana Siegel, Alane Siem, Alanna D., Alina Kasper, Alejandra Echenagucia, Alejandro Toscano, Aleksandra Sedova, Alena Brandenburg, Alex Caspescha, Alexander Ferstl, Alexandra Ambrico, Alexandra Crowley, Alexandra Kern, Alexandra Zoicas, Aline Kinas, Alisa Grechenok, Alison Reddie, Alison Cokorinos, Alison Kent, Alison Lowy, Alix Schönwald, Alma Nathanaili, Alyona Nagel, Alžběta, Amanda Mancia, Amanda Steinhardt, Amelia Anair, Amélie Maire, Amelie Schwierholz, Amethyst Mantha, Amy Harcourt, Amy Maynard, Amy Monro Henderson, Amy Oliver And Family, Ana Castillo de Amaya, Ana Chirilova, Ana Estrella, Ana Maria Polley Grigore, Ana Posada, Ana Preciado, Ana Stadelwieser, Anastasia Correa, André Ramos Moreno De Souza, Andrea David, Andrea Gutierrez, Andrea Kläsener, Andrea Thomson, Andreea Balici, Andrew Kemp, Anela Vale, Angela Portwood, Angelika Lux, Angelika Pinisch, Angelique Regnier-Golanov, Ania Szuminska, Anita Buchetmann, Anita Kolb, Anja Bomberg, Anna Cicozi, Anna Colombo, Anna Kurwinkel, Anna Lentzsch And Tim Handzel, Anna Schley, Anne Haas, Anne Jakymyszyn, Anne-Christine Kramm, Anne-Laure Terrin, Annette Lenz, Annie Ho, Annika Brand, Anouk Van Zandvoort, Anthony PM, Antia Perez-Blackwell, Antje Konnerth, Anusha, Arianna Buzzini, Artiola Çollaku, Ashley Bonaventura, Ashley Brown, Ashley Westerback, Astrid Spek, Audrey Ch., Babette Heller, Barbara Church, Barbara Jongbloed, Barbara Peters, Barbara Syrowatka, Beau Wilson, Benedikte Andersen, Bertine Uithoven, Betsy Purves, Bianca Urieș, Bianka Szabo, Blanca Capraro, Brette Shealy, Brianna, Britta, Bronwyn Mednick, Caitlin Allen, Cali Luco, Carine Biolé, Carla Bernardes, Carla Teixeira, Carley Lovell, Carly Williams, Carmen Maria Navarron Izquierdo, Carmen Tauber, Carol McAloney, Carole Giunta, Caroline Chretien, Caroline Forster, Caroline Meyer Thivierge, Carson Massey, Catarina Preto, Catharina Kauffmann, Catherine Pouliot, Cathy Lavelle, Cecilie Munoz, Celina Bertero, Chanel Di Giacomo, Charles Teague, Charlotte Fléchon, Chirine Merien, Chloe Rew, Chris Beischel, Christiane S., Claire Mallet, Clara Thompson, Claudette d'Argent, Claudia Pivaral, Clémence Coiffe, Clémentine Beyens, Cornelia Siem, Cyrine Dufaux, Dana Hentges Sheridan, Daniela Solís Adolio, Daniella Novak, Danielle Lajoie, Darina Puricelli, Darya K., David Dederer, Debora Menahem, Deborah Ramsay, Denize Aller, Desire Uzal Botana, Desislava Tsekova, Diana Albergaria, Diana Duque, Dimitra Neufert, Dominika Pydych, Donny Mckendall, Donovan Cormier, Dori Bregaj, Doriane Marchal, Dorota & Maciej, Dragos Popa, Duygu Jones, Edita Blaha, Eduardo Tabe, Ekaterina Antoniuk, Elaine Goldenberg, Elin Hagen, Elisa Klabunde, Elisabeth Anderson, Elisabeth Gebel, Elisabeth Oesch, Elisabetta Maria Zocca, Eliska Hortova, Elizabeth Keaton, Elizabeth Krebs, Elke Ortner, Elliot Barnett, Elsa Le Menthéour, Elsa Scremin, Elva Sarmiento, Emily Barnes, Emily Owen, Emily Reichenbach, Emily Rommelman, Emma Hausfeld, Emmy Souka, Eric Tully, Esmeralda Tafani, Esther Kott, Eugenia Martinez Jaime, Eva-Maria, Evgeniia Larionova, Fabien Guillot, Fabienne Conte, Fabienne Chauveau, Fabienne S., Facon Pauline, Fatima Alremeithi, Faustine Massin, Federica Filomena, Fernanda Sequeira, Fiona von Vaernewyck, Flora Garnier, Flora Nevers, Franca Flabiano, Frances Novak, Francesca Romana Achilles, Franz Rast, Gabriela Ivanova, Gabriela Toviah, Gary Cook, Gemma Neil, Georges Dejean, Georgina Coupland, Georgina Griffin, Geraldine Bornholdt, Géraldine Chotard, Geraldine Galka, Geraldine Marshall-Hine, Géraldine Lüthi, Gianna Gibo, Gilles Herve, Gimena Finocchi, Gina Benavente, Gina Heintzelmann, Giovanna Fois, Glenna Valverde,

Grazyna Wilczkiewicz, Greta Alschner, Gwen Armstrong, Hanna Mirska, Hannah Böker, Hannah Fellechner, Heather Ragoonanan, Helen Beckner, Helen Sonnemans, Hilles Whedbee, Ilona Kraukle, Inga Link, Ingrid Raynaud, Irena Marceta, Irene Cayuela, Iris Raiford, Isabel Caniço, Isabel Friedenberg, Iulia Simba, Iuliia Weber, Iva Stankova, Jana Anhamm, Jana Sporin, Jane Delaney, Janet Gregory, Janice Chumakov, Jasmijn Rabbering, Jasminka D., Jay Hiers, Jayna Rana, Jeannie Natasha, Jeannine Scheff, Jennifer Manzo, Jennifer McAmis-Rich, Jennifer Wendl, Jessica Hallowes, Jessica Marquez, Jessica O'Leary-Vaccaro, Jessica-Mae Robertson, Jim Wahlen, Joana Carvalho, Joanna Leung, Joanne Cortese, Jocelyn Ahern, Johanna Esser, Jonas Kolpin, Jose Soto, Josefina Reynal Morandé, Josephine Purcell, Josue Carriera, Joy Felter, Joy Souza, Juanice Oldham, Julia Ambs, Julia Grys, Julia Gürtler, Julia Mitterbauer, Julia Schwarze, Julia Zrąbkowska, Julian Bug, Juliette Janssen, Justine Berardet Van Ruymbeke, Karen Mcdowall, Karen Menezes, Karin Gubler, Karolina Radko, Katarina Gligovic, Kate Blanchard, Kate Byrne, Kate Law, Kate Salter, Kathryn Gerth, Katibe Paris, Katie Schwausch, Katie Stiles, Keilit Bauer, Kelly Mccain And Vincent Maffet, Kelsey Donegan Jessup, Kelsey Laderriere, Kenneth Mcmahan, Kerri Alexander, Kim Dutton, Kim Dutton, Kimberley Smith, Kirsten Christophersen, Klára Náhlíková, Koleta Jankowski, Konstanze Kühn, Kristina Nassiri, Krisztina Bobak, Ksenia Kazymova Vasiliadis, Laura B., Laura Calendo, Laura Dauban, Laura Göbel, Laura Hann, Laura Hegwood, Laura Kok, Laura Martínez García, Laura Quigley, Laura Studer, Lauren Reichstein, Laurene Courillon, Laurie Dunston, Léa Hinzelin, Lea Morris, Leah Neeson, Léana Prampart, Leila Zuñiga, Lena Blomberg, Lena Lödel, Lena Schmitz, Leni Bauer, Leo, Léonie Depoix, Leonie Lüdemann, Letisha Evita Pereira, Letizia Rocca, Lex Wick, Lidia-Marta Amarandi-Netedu, Liesbeth Wouters, Lilia Rivera, Lilia S. Torres, Lilli Lu Riedel, Lindsey Burridge, Lisa Autzen, Lisa Clayton, Lisa Janofsky, Lisa Kogler, Lisa Sullivan, Lisa Taylor, Lisa Tönnies, Lisa Yde, Listya Kusumawati, Liza Bernstein, Loes Schoenmakers, Logan Moriarty, Loraine Delaporte, Loren Di Molfetta, Lorenz Kemper, Lori Y., Lorraine Gasser Bensoussan, Lou Fouchard, Luca Rossi, Lucas Hale, Lucie Leclercq, Lucinda Pearson, Lucy Anderson, Luis Perches, Luisa Höfler, Luisiana Zappa, Lutza Holster, Luz Alvarez, Luz Ruiz-Tagle, Lydia Sizemore, Lynda Messer, Madeline Snyder, Maëva, Magda U., Magda W., Maja Kunčič, Makayla Mccoy, Maline, Manjola Salla, Manon Vacher, Manuela Bassetti, Manuela Rees, Margaret Lagimodiere, Margarita Dolgener, Mari Luist, Maria Luigi, Maria Makunina, Maria Montoya, Marian Lichtenegger, Marianela Manzione, Marianella Zamora, Marianna Boutopoulou, Marie A., Marie Aude Leroux, Marie Dechant, Marie Frey, Marie Nowack, Marie-Anne Reiter, Marie Esther, Marieke Van Leeuwen, Marine Vallet, Marion Heimbürger, Markus Müller-Van Heek, Martin Goffeney, Martina Hofmann, Mary Antaki, Maryline Leva, Maryna Popova, Mathilde Hamon, Mathilde Sivignolle, Matthew Lee, Matthew Medina, Maya Ayache, Mayte Palomares, Medina Avdagic, Meena Reddi, Megan Clifford, Mel Cahill, Mélanie Philippi, Melanie Scharr, Mélissa Brys, Michael Serbousek, Michele Thompson, Michelle Enns, Michelle Mannino, Michelle Twardzik, Michelle Vega Mauser, Milana Foulon, Milica Oliver Alfonso, Mira Maalouf, Mira Peters, Miriam Givoni, Mirja Weidemann, Mirsad Dizdarević, Missy & John Villapudua, Molly Haggerty, Moritz Thiel, Myriam Jacobs, Myriam Jacobs, Myriam Van De Velde, Nadia Le Divenach, Nadia Nasevich, Nancy Drader, Naomi Codrean, Natalia Gerenschtein, Natalia Kritskaya, Natalia Kunzer, Nataliia Bucholtz, Nataliya Mishukova, Natasha Tagasovska, Nathalie Chambers, Nathaniel Arsenault, Naz Dursunoğlu, Neele Barthel, Nena Olsavova, Nermin Prodanovic, Neža Pogačar, Nick Denyer, Nicola Welz, Nicole Woods, Niki Pretorius,

Niklas Schäfer, Niklas Sujan, Nina Dannell, Nina & Philipp Korfmann, Nina Rummel (Soon Eckard), Nisha, Noémi Anna Galazek (& Paul Duscha), Noémie Virollaud, Noreen Raper, Noviana Marseline, Oksana Pigina, Pablo Rosenthal-Almirall, Paige Lathrope, Paloma Pardo, Pamela Tremblay, Paola Canty, Paola Fischer, Paula Montemuro, Paula Scharf, Paula Galhardo Teixeira, Paulina Moser-Hofer, Pauline Lambert, Pauline L., Penny Roberts, Pernille Rosendahl, Persia Nicolaou, Philipp Steingrebe, Philippe Teuscher, Polona Ramšak, Pratheeksha Abiram, Rachel Pallas, Rachel Bradshaw, Rachel Unruh, Ramona Balc, Raphael Schmid, Raya Stefanova, Ricarda Newton-Schauwinhold, Rita Humeau, Rita Kyurklyan, Roberto, Robin Conner, Robin Taher, Robin Vilkas, Robyl Albacite, Romain Hameau, Rosa Garcia Fernandez, Rosalie Acinapura, Rosio Garcia, Roxane Chardon, Rumyana Dimitrova, Ryan Camilleri, Ryan Camilleri, Samantha Nicole, Samara, Samira Bravo Ortega, Sandra Johnson, Sandra Mellem Enoksen, Sangita Baxi, Sapir Korman Shadmi, Sara Rapic, Sarah Burns, Sarah Dali, Sarah Décarpentrie, Sarah Farrell, Sarah Fox, Sarah Grant, Sarah Haigh, Sarah Schlechtriem, Sarah Zielke, Saskia Zijlstra, Scott Ensley, Semra Gulder, Serge Ledashchev, Serina Dabbah, Sevda Boyanova, Sharon Jung, Shawn Mitchell, Shawna Batty, Sheila Litman, Sheldon Veeran, Sibylla Degen, Silia Schapals, Silvia Stecher, Silviya Parsadanyan, Siobhán Parker, Sitraka Rasolofo, Sonja Van Praag, Sophie Hermans, Stacey Snacks, Stephan Shurn, Stéphane Vadez, Stephanie P.A., Stephanie Gathmann, Stephen and Nora Ingram, Sue Oxford, Suellen Leite Freire, Sumeyra Aydogan, Susan Stott, Susan Tilney, Suzan Krauland, Suzanne Batson, Sylvain Bremaud, Sylvie Jannon-Shields, Tamar Van Meer, Tamara Voigt, Tamara Wilson, Tanya Jackson, Tara Trimble, Taylor Weibert, Temida Novak, Teresa Ehl, Tetiana Tanina, Theresa Gatzen, Thomas Wright, Tiffany Lobner, Tina Harris, Tiphaine Verhooghe, Titta Kuokkanen, Toni Little, Tori Meadows, Tracey Balsdon, Trisha Mackenzie, Trixia Chrisholm, Tu Vuong, Tyler Waneka, Valentin Rubin, Valerie Odet, Vanessa Bilh, Vanessa Risch, Vanessa Wasserrab, Vera Hörauf, Vera Hüllenkremer, Veronika Hövel, Vicki Swinson, Vicky Baraldi, Vicky Becart, Victoria Hun, Vrinda Gulati, Wafa Slimi, Wendy Ohlson, Wendy Sullivan, Wiebke Hensgen, Wouter Jobse, Yarden Even Chen, Yasemin Özkan, Yasmin Clara, Yvonne Neeser, Zina Herman, Zoe Lane, Zuzana Ménard, Zuzanna Czerczak

INDEX

© 2025 by Quarto Publishing Group USA, Inc.
Text and Photography © 2025 by Géraldine Leverd

First published in 2025 by Rock Point,
an imprint of The Quarto Group,
142 West 36th Street, 4th Floor,
New York, NY 10018, USA
(212) 779-4972 www.Quarto.com

Rock Point titles are also available at discount for retail, wholesale, promotional and bulk purchase. For details, contact the Special Sales Manager by email at specialsales@quarto.com or by mail at The Quarto Group, Attn: Special Sales Manager, 100 Cummings Center Suite, 265D, Beverly, MA 01915, USA.

10 9 8 7 6 5 4 3 2 1

ISBN: 978-1-57715-475-4

Digital edition published in 2025
eISBN: 978-0-7603-9287-4

Library of Congress Cataloging-in-Publication Data

Names: Leverd, Géraldine, author.
Title: The new French kitchen : modern takes on favorite classic dishes / Géraldine Leverd.
Description: New York, NY, USA : Rock Point, 2025. | Includes index. | Summary: "The New French Kitchen demystifies the art of French cooking with 75 sensuous recipes featuring fresh, easy-to-find ingredients and modern cooking techniques"— Provided by publisher.
Identifiers: LCCN 2024041834 (print) | LCCN 2024041835 (ebook) | ISBN 9781577154754 (hardcover) | ISBN 9780760392874 (ebook)
Subjects: LCSH: Cooking, French. | LCGFT: Cookbooks.
Classification: LCC TX719 .L4847 2025 (print) | LCC TX719 (ebook) | DDC 641.5944–dc23/eng/20240923
LC record available at https://lccn.loc.gov/2024041834
LC ebook record available at https://lccn.loc.gov/2024041835

Publisher: Rage Kindelsperger
Creative Director: Laura Drew
Senior Art Director: Marisa Kwek
Editorial Director: Erin Canning
Managing Editor: Cara Donaldson
Cover and Interior Design: Tara Long

Printed in China